Rick Steves' ®
SNAPSHOT

Normandy

CONTENTS

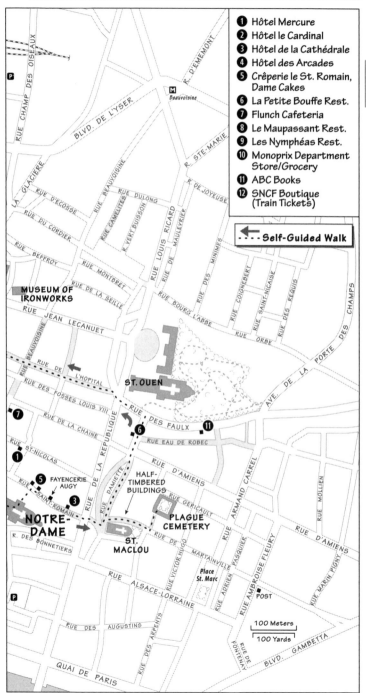

1 Hôtel Mercure
2 Hôtel le Cardinal
3 Hôtel de la Cathédrale
4 Hôtel des Arcades
5 Crêperie le St. Romain, Dame Cakes
6 La Petite Bouffe Rest.
7 Flunch Cafeteria
8 Le Maupassant Rest.
9 Les Nymphéas Rest.
10 Monoprix Department Store/Grocery
11 ABC Books
12 SNCF Boutique (Train Tickets)

← - - - **Self-Guided Walk**

The Hundred Years' War (1336-1453)

It would take a hundred years to explain all the causes, battles, and political maneuverings of this century-plus of warfare between France and England, but here goes:

In 1300, before the era of the modern nation-state, the borders between France and England were fuzzy. French-speaking kings had ruled England, English kings owned the south of France, and English merchants dominated trade in the north. Dukes and lords in both countries were aligned more along family lines than by national identity. When the French king died without a male heir (1328), both France and England claimed the crown, and the battle was on.

England invaded the more populous country (1345) and—thanks to skilled archers using armor-penetrating longbows—won big battles at Crécy (1346) and Poitiers (1356). Despite a truce, roving bands of English mercenaries stayed behind and supported themselves by looting French villages. The French responded with guerrilla tactics.

In 1415, the English took still more territory, with Henry V's big victory at Agincourt. But rallied by the heavenly visions of young Joan of Arc, the French slowly drove the invaders out. Paris was liberated in 1436, and when Bordeaux fell to French forces (1453), the fighting ended without a treaty.

14:00). This walk is designed for day-trippers coming by train. Drivers should park at or near Place du Vieux Marché (parking garages available).

From Place du Vieux Marché, you'll walk the length of Rue du Gros Horloge to Notre-Dame Cathedral. From there, walk four blocks to the plague cemetery (Aître St. Maclou), loop up to the church of St. Ouen, and return along Rue de l'Hôpital ending at the Museum of Fine Arts (a 5-minute walk to the train station).

• *If arriving by train, walk down Rue Jeanne d'Arc and turn right on Rue du Guillaume le Conquérant (notice the Gothic Palace of Justice building across Rue Jeanne d'Arc—we'll get to that later). This takes you to the back door of our starting point...*

Place du Vieux Marché

• *Stand near the entrance of the striking Joan of Arc Church.*

Surrounded by half-timbered buildings, this old market square has a covered produce market, a park commemorating Joan of Arc's burning, and a modern church named after her. A tall aluminum cross, planted in a flowery garden near the church entry, marks the spot where Rouen publicly punished and executed people. The pillories stood here, and during the Revolution, the town's guillotine made 800 people "a foot shorter at the top." In

1431, Joan of Arc—only 19 years old—was burned at this site. Find her flaming statue facing the cross. As the flames engulfed her, an English soldier said, "Oh my God, we've killed a saint." (Nearly 500 years later, Joan was canonized, and the soldier was proved right.)

▲▲Joan of Arc Church (Eglise Jeanne d'Arc)

This modern church is a tribute to the young woman who was canonized in 1920 and later became the patron saint of France. The church, completed in 1979, feels Scandinavian inside and out—another reminder of Normandy's Nordic roots. Sumptuous 16th-century windows, salvaged from a church lost during World War II, were worked into the soft architectural lines (the €0.50 English pamphlet provides some background and describes the stained-glass scenes). Similar to modern churches designed by the 20th-century architect Le Corbusier, this is an uplifting place to be, with a ship's-hull vaulting and sweeping wood ceiling that sail over curved pews and a wall of glass below. Make time to savor this unusual place.

Cost and Hours: Free; Mon-Thu and Sat 10:00-12:00 & 14:00-18:00, Fri and Sun 14:00-17:30; closed during Mass. A public WC is 30 yards straight ahead from the church doors.

• *Turn left out of the church and step over the ruins of a 15th-century church that once stood on this spot (destroyed during the French Revolution). Leave the square and join the busy pedestrian street, Rue du Gros Horloge—the town's main shopping street since Roman times. A block up on your right (at #163) is Rouen's most famous chocolate shop...*

Les Larmes de Jeanne d'Arc

The chocolate-makers of Les Larmes de Jeanne d'Arc would love to tempt you with their chocolate-covered almond "tears *(larmes)* of Joan of Arc." Although you must resist touching the chocolate fountain, you are welcome to taste a tear. The first one is free; a small bag costs about €8 (Mon-Sat 9:00-19:00, closed Sun).

• *Your route continues past a medieval McDonald's and across busy Rue Jeanne d'Arc to the...*

▲Big Clock (Gros Horloge)

This impressive, circa-1528 Renaissance clock, le Gros Horloge (groh oar-lohzh), decorates the former City Hall. Is something missing? Not really. In the 16th century, an hour hand offered sufficient precision; minute hands became necessary only in a later, faster-paced age. The lamb at the end of the hour hand is a reminder that wool rules—it was the source of Rouen's wealth. The town medallion features a sacrificial lamb, which has both religious and commercial significance (center, below the clock).

NORMANDY

Joan of Arc (1412-1431)

The cross-dressing teenager who rallied French soldiers to drive out English invaders was the illiterate daughter of a humble farmer. One summer day, in her dad's garden, 13-year-old Joan heard a heavenly voice accompanied by bright light. It was the first of several saints (including Michael, Margaret, and Catherine) to talk to her during her short life.

In 1429, the young girl was instructed by the voices to save France from the English. Dressed in men's clothing, she traveled to see the king and predicted that the French armies would be defeated near Orléans—as they were. King Charles VII equipped her with an ancient sword and a banner that read "Jesus, Maria," and sent her to rally the troops.

Soon "the Maid" *(la Pucelle)* was bivouacking amid rough soldiers, riding with them into battle, and suffering an arrow wound to the chest—all while liberating the town of Orléans. On July 17, 1429, she held her banner high in the cathedral of Reims as Charles was officially proclaimed king of a resurgent France.

Joan and company next tried to retake Paris (1429), but the English held out. She suffered a crossbow wound through the thigh, and her reputation of invincibility was tarnished. During a battle at Compiègne (1430), she was captured and turned over to the English for £10,000. The English took her to Rouen where she was chained by the neck inside an iron cage, while the local French authorities (allied with the English) plotted against her. The Inquisition—insisting that Joan's voices were "false and diabolical"—tried and sentenced her to death for being a witch and a heretic.

On May 30, 1431, Joan of Arc was tied to a stake on Rouen's old market square (Place du Vieux Marché). She yelled, "Rouen! Rouen! Must I die here?" Then they lit the fire; she fixed her eyes on a crucifix and died chanting, "Jesus, Jesus, Jesus."

After her death, Joan's place in history was slowly rehabilitated. French authorities proclaimed her trial illegal (1455), prominent writers and artists were inspired by her, and the Catholic Church finally beatified (1909) and canonized her (1920) as St. Joan of Arc.

The silver orb above the clock makes one revolution in 29 days. The clock's artistic highlight fills the underside of the arch (walk underneath and stretch your back), with the "Good Shepherd" and loads of sheep.

To see the inner workings and an extraordinary panorama over Rouen (including a stirring view of the cathedral), climb the clock tower's 100 steps. You'll tour several rooms with the help of an audioguide that suffers from a Goldilocks-and-the-Three-Bears narration. The big bells ring on the hour—a deafening experience if you're in the tower.

Cost and Hours: €6, includes audioguide; April-Oct Tue-Sun 10:00-12:00 & 13:00-18:00; Nov-March Tue-Sun 14:00-18:00; closed Mon year-round.

• *Walk under le Gros Horloge, then take a one-block detour left on Rue Thouret to see the...*

Palace of Justice (Palais de Justice)

Years of cleaning have removed the grime that once covered this fabulously flamboyantly Gothic building, the former home of Normandy's *parlement* and the largest civil Gothic building in France. The result is striking; think of this as you visit Rouen's other Gothic structures; some are awaiting baths of their own. Pockmarks on the side of the building that faces Rue Jeanne d'Arc are leftovers from bombings during the Normandy invasion. Look for the English-language plaques on the iron fence—they provide some history, and describe the damage and tedious repair process.

• *Double back and continue up Rue du Gros Horloge. In a block you'll see a stone plaque dedicated to Cavelier de la Salle (high on the left), who explored the mouth of the Mississippi River, claimed the state of Louisiana for France, and was assassinated in Texas in 1687. Soon you'll reach...*

▲▲Notre-Dame Cathedral (Cathédrale Notre-Dame)

This cathedral is a landmark of art history. You're seeing essentially what Claude Monet saw as he painted 30 different studies of this frilly Gothic facade at various times of the day. Using the physical building only as a rack upon which to hang light, mist, dusk, and shadows, Monet was capturing "impressions." One of the results is in Rouen's Museum of Fine Arts; four others are at the Orsay Museum in Paris. Find the plaque showing two of these paintings (in the corner of the square, about 30 paces to your right if you were exiting the TI).

Cost and Hours: Free, Tue-Sun 8:00-19:00, Mon 14:00-19:00; closed during Mass Tue-Sat at 10:00, July-Aug also at 18:00, Sun and holidays at 8:30, 10:30, and 12:00; also closed Nov-March daily 12:00-14:00.

Cathedral Exterior: There's been a church on this site since the fourth century. Charlemagne honored it with a visit in the eighth century before the Vikings sacked it a hundred years later. The building you see today was constructed between the 12th and 14th centuries, though lightning strikes, wars (the cathedral was devastated in WWII fighting), and other destructive forces meant constant rebuilding—which explains the difference in the towers, such as the stones used at each tower's base.

Look up at the soaring facade and find the cleaned sections, with bright statues on either side of the central portal—later, we'll meet some of their friends face to face inside the cathedral. The facade is another fine Rouen example of Flamboyant Gothic, and the spire, soaring nearly 500 feet high, is awe-inspiring. Why such a big cathedral here? Until the 1700s, Rouen was the second-largest city in France—rich from its wool trade and its booming port.

Cathedral Interior: Stand at the back and look down the **nave.** This is a classic Gothic nave—four stories of pointed-arch arcades, the top filled with windows to help light the interior. Today, the interior is lighter than intended, because the original colored glass (destroyed mostly in World War II) was replaced by clear glass.

Circle counterclockwise around the church along the side aisle. The side chapels and windows have short descriptions in English, each dedicated to a different saint. These chapels display the changing assortment of styles through the centuries. Look for photos halfway down on the right that show WWII bomb damage to the cathedral, then find an impressive display of the damage and eventual reconstruction.

Passing through an iron gate after the high altar (closed during Mass; may be open on the opposite side even during Mass), you come to several **stone statues.** These figures were lifted from the facade during a cleaning and should eventually be installed in a museum. For us, it's a rare chance to stand toe-to-toe with a saint (weird feeling).

There are several **stone tombs** on your left, dating from when Rouen was the Norman capital. The first tomb is for Rollo, the first duke of Normandy in 933 (and great-great-great-great grandfather of William the Conqueror, seventh duke of Normandy, c. 1028). As the first duke, Rollo was chief of the first gang of Vikings (the original "Normans") who decided to settle here. Called the "Father of Normandy," Rollo died at the age of 80, but he is portrayed on his tomb as if he were 33 (as was the fashion, because Jesus died at that age). Because of later pillage and plunder, only Rollo's femur is inside the tomb.

And speaking of body parts, the next tomb contains the heart of Richard the Lionhearted. (The rest of his body lies in the Abbey of Fontevraud.) A descendant of William the Conqueror, Richard was both a king of England and the 12th duke of Normandy.

Circle behind the altar. The beautiful **windows** with bold blues and reds are generally from the 13th century. Look back above the entry to see a rare black-and-white rose window (its medieval colored glass is long gone). You'll come to a display for the window dedicated to St. Julien, with pane-by-pane descriptions in English.

Continue a few paces, then look up to the **ceiling** over the nave. Looking directly above Rollo's femur on the opposite side of the apse, you can see the patchwork in the ceiling where the spire crashed through the roof. Perhaps this might be a good time to exit? Pass through the small iron gate, turn right, and leave through the side door (north transept).

Stepping outside, look back at the **facade** over the door. The fine carved tympanum (the area over the door) shows a graphic Last Judgment. Jesus stands between the saved (on the left) and the damned (on the right). Notice the devil grasping a miser, who clutches a bag of coins. Look for the hellish hot tub, where even a bishop (pointy hat) is eternally in hot water. And is it my imagination, or are those saved souls on the far right high-fiving each other?

Most of the facade has been cleaned—blasted with jets of water—but the limestone carving is still black. It's too delicate to survive the hosing. A more expensive laser cleaning has begun, and the result is astonishing.

• *From this courtyard, a gate deposits you on a traffic-free street. Turn right and walk along...*

Rue St. Romain

This street has half-timbered buildings and lanes worth a look. In a short distance, you can look through an arch, back at the cathedral's prickly spire. Made of cast iron in the late 1800s—about the same time Gustave Eiffel was building his tower in Paris—the spire is, at 490 feet, the tallest in France. You can also see the former location of the missing smaller (green) spire—downed in a violent 1999 storm that blew the spire off the roof and sent it crashing to the cathedral floor.

• *Farther down the street, find a shop that shows off a traditional art form in action.*

At **Fayencerie Augy** (at #26), Monsieur Augy and his staff welcome shoppers to browse his studio/gallery/shop and see Rouen's clay "china" being made the traditional way. First, the clay is molded and fired. Then it's dipped in white enamel, dried, lovingly hand-painted, and fired a second time. Rouen was the first city in France to make faience, earthenware with colored glazes. In the 1700s, the town had 18 factories churning out the popular product (Mon-Sat 9:00-19:00, closed Sun, 26 Rue St. Romain, VAT tax refunds nearly pay for the shipping, www.fayencerie-augy.com). For more faience, visit the local Museum of Ceramics (described later, under "Sights in Rouen").

• *Continue along Rue St. Romain, which (after crossing Rue de la Ré-publique) leads to the fancy...*

St. Maclou Church

This church's unique, bowed facade is textbook Flamboyant Goth-ic. Its recent cleaning (still underway) revealed a brilliant white fa-cade. Notice the flame-like tracery decorating its gable. Because this was built at the very end of the Gothic age—and construction took many years—the doors are from the next age: the Renaissance (c. 1550). The bright and airy interior is worth a quick peek.

Cost and Hours: Free, Fri-Mon 10:00-12:00 & 14:00-17:30, closed Tue-Thu.

• *Leaving the church, turn right, and then take another right (giving the little boys on the corner wall a wide berth). Wander past a fine wall of half-timbered buildings fronting Rue Martainville, to the end of St. Maclou Church.*

Half-Timbered Buildings

Because the local stone—a chalky limestone from the cliffs of the Seine River—was of poor quality (your thumbnail is stronger), and because local oak was plentiful, half-timbered buildings became a Rouen specialty from the 14th through 19th century. Cantilevered floors were standard until the early 1500s. These top-heavy designs made sense: City land was limited, property taxes were based on ground-floor square footage, and the cantilevering minimized unsupported spans on upper floors. The oak beams provided the structural skeleton of the building, which was then filled in with a mix of clay, straw, pebbles...or whatever was available.

• *A block farther down on the left, at 186 Rue Martainville, a covered lane leads to the...*

Plague Cemetery (Aître St. Maclou)

During the great plagues of the Middle Ages, as many as two-thirds of the people in this parish died. For the decimated commu-nity, dealing with the corpses was an overwhelming task. This half-timbered courtyard (c. 1520) was a mass grave, an ossuary where the bodies were "processed." Bodies would be dumped into the grave (where the well is now) and drenched in liquid lime to help speed decomposition. Later, the bones would be stacked in alcoves above the colonnades that line this courtyard. Notice the ghoulish carv-ings (c. 1560s) of gravediggers' tools, skulls, crossbones, and char-acters doing the "dance of death." In this *danse macabre*, Death, the great equalizer, grabs people of all social classes. The place is now an art school. Peek in on the young artists. As you leave, spy the dried black cat (died c. 1520, in tiny glass case to the left of the door). To overcome evil, it was buried during the building's construction.

Cost and Hours: Free, daily mid-March-Oct 8:00-20:00, Nov-mid-March 8:00-19:00.

Nearby: Farther down Rue Martainville, at Place St. Marc, a colorful market blooms Sunday until about 12:30 and all day Tuesday, Friday, and Saturday. If it's not market day, you can double back to the cathedral and Rue du Gros Horloge, or continue with me to explore more of Rouen and find the Museum of Fine Arts (back toward the train station).

NORMANDY

• *To reach the museum, turn right upon leaving the boneyard, then right again at the little boys (onto Rue Damiette), and hike up antique row to the vertical St. Ouen Church (a seventh-century abbey turned church in the 15th century, fine park behind). Turn left at the church on Rue des Faulx (an English-language bookstore, ABC Books, is a block to the right), and cross the busy street. (The horseman you see to the right is a short yet majestic Napoleon Bonaparte, who welcomes visitors to Rouen's City Hall.)*

*Continue down Rue de l'Hôpital's traffic-free lane, which becomes Rue Ganterie (admire the Gothic fountain at Rue Beauvoisine). A right at the modern square on Rue de l'Ecureuil leads you to the **Museum of Fine Arts** and the **Museum of Ironworks** (both described next, under "Sights in Rouen"). This is the end of our tour. The tower where Joan of Arc was imprisoned (also explained later) is a few blocks uphill, on the way back to the train station.*

Sights in Rouen

The first three museums are within a block of one another, closed on Tuesdays, never crowded, and can all be visited with the same €8 combo-ticket (www.rouen-musees.com).

▲Museum of Fine Arts (Musée des Beaux-Arts)

Paintings from many periods are beautifully displayed in this overlooked two-floor museum, including works by Caravaggio, Peter Paul Rubens, Paolo Veronese, Jan Steen, Théodore Géricault, Jean-Auguste-Dominique Ingres, Eugène Delacroix, and several Impressionists. With its reasonable entry fee and calm interior, this museum is worth a short visit for the Impressionists and a surgical hit of a few other key artists. The museum café is good for a peaceful break from the action outside.

Cost and Hours: €5, occasional temporary exhibitions cost extra, €8 combo-ticket includes ironworks and ceramics museums; open Wed-Mon 10:00-18:00, 15th-17th-century rooms closed 13:00-14:00, closed Tue; a few blocks below train station at 26 bis Rue Jean Lecanuet, tel. 02 35 71 28 40.

Visiting the Museum: Pick up the essential museum map at the ticket desk. Climb the stairs to the upper floor, where you'll focus your time and savor the complete lack of crowds. Find the excellent handheld English descriptions in key rooms. There's a gallery dedicated to Géricault and a good collection of Ingres' work (smaller paintings than at the Louvre, but worth a look). In the next rooms you'll find scenes inspired by Normandy's landscape—painted by Impressionists Monet, Sisley, and Pissarro—and a handful of paintings from Renoir, Degas, and Corot. Room 2.25 showcases a must-see scene of Rouen's busy port in 1855.

Other rooms on the upper floor are devoted to French painters from the 17th and 18th centuries (Boucher, Fragonard, and Poussin) and Italian works, including several by Veronese. A gripping Caravaggio canvas, depicting the flagellation of Christ, demands attention with its dramatic lighting and realistic faces.

Back on the ground floor, pass through the bookstore to find an intriguing collection of backlit panels created in homage to hometown boy Marcel Duchamp. Several colorful Modiglianis and one grand-scale Delacroix are nearby.

Museum of Ironworks (Musée le Secq des Tournelles, a.k.a. Musée de la Ferronnerie)

This deconsecrated church houses iron objects, many of them more than 1,500 years old. Locks, chests, keys, tools, thimbles, coffee grinders, corkscrews, and flatware from centuries ago—virtually anything made of iron is on display. You can duck into the entry area for a glimpse of a medieval iron scene without passing through the turnstile.

Cost and Hours: €3, €8 combo-ticket includes fine arts and ceramics museums, no English explanations—bring a French/English dictionary, Wed-Mon 14:00-18:00, closed Tue, behind Museum of Fine Arts, 2 Rue Jacques Villon, tel. 02 35 88 42 92.

Museum of Ceramics (Musée de la Céramique)

Rouen's famous faience (earthenware), which dates from the 16th to 18th century, fills this fine old mansion. There's not a word of English except in the museum leaflet.

Cost and Hours: €3, €8 combo-ticket includes fine arts and ironworks museums, Wed-Mon 14:00-18:00, closed Tue, 1 Rue Faucon, tel. 02 35 07 31 74.

Joan of Arc Tower (Le Tour Jeanne d'Arc)

This massive tower (1204), part of Rouen's brooding castle, was Joan's prison before her untimely death. Cross the deep moat and find three small floors (and 122 spiral steps) covering tidbits of Rouen's and Joan's history, well-described in English. The top floor gives a good peek at an impressive wood substructure but no views.

Cost and Hours: €1.50, Wed-Sat and Mon 10:00-12:30 & 14:00-18:00, Sun 14:00-18:30, closed Tue, one block uphill from the Museum of Fine Arts on Rue du Bouvreuil, tel. 02 35 98 16 21.

Near Rouen

The Route of the Ancient Abbeys
(La Route des Anciennes Abbayes)

This route—punctuated with abbeys, apples, and Seine River views—provides a pleasing detour for drivers connecting Rouen and destinations farther west (if you're traveling *sans* car, skip it). Follow D-982 west of Rouen to Jumièges (visit its abbey), then cross the Seine on the car ferry at Duclair (about €2).

Drivers can stop to admire the gleaming Romanesque church at the **Abbey of St. Georges de Boscherville** (but skip the abbey grounds). The romantically ruined twin-towered **Abbey of Jumièges** is the top sight to visit on this route. Founded in A.D. 654, it was destroyed by Vikings and rebuilt by William the Conqueror, only to be torn down again by French Revolutionaries who used it as a quarry. Today there is no roof to protect the abbey, but the French are carefully conserving what's left as an evocative ruin. Because it's off the tourist track, you'll have this magical medieval sight to yourself—it's worth the detour (€6, iPad videoguide-€5, helpful English handout, more detailed booklet for sale, daily mid-April–mid-Sept 9:30-18:30, mid-Sept-mid-April 9:30-13:00 & 14:30-17:30, last entry 30 minutes before closing, tel. 02 35 37 24 02, www.abbayedejumieges.fr). Several decent lunch options lie across the street from the abbey.

Sleeping in Rouen

Although I prefer Rouen by day, sleeping here presents you with a mostly tourist-free city (most hotels cater to business travelers). These hotels are perfectly central, within two blocks of Notre-Dame Cathedral.

$$$ Hôtel Mercure*, ideally situated a block north of the cathedral, is a concrete business hotel with a professional staff, a comfortable lobby and bar, and 125 rooms loaded with modern comforts. Suites come with views of the cathedral, but are pricey and not much bigger than a double. Look for big discounts online (standard Db-€120-160, "privilege" Db-€160-200, suite-€290, breakfast-€17, air-con, elevator, guest computer, free Wi-Fi, parking garage-€13/day, 7 Rue Croix de Fer, tel. 02 35 52 69 52, www.mercure.com, h1301@accor.com).

$$$ Hôtel le Cardinal** is a sharp place with handsome rooms, most with point-blank views of the cathedral and all with queen-size beds and spacious bathrooms (standard Db-€90-115; €140-160 for fourth-floor rooms—the hotel's largest, with balconies and great cathedral views; non-smoking rooms available, breakfast-€9, elevator, Wi-Fi, 1 Place de la Cathédrale, tel. 02 35

Sleep Code

(€1 = $1.30, country code: 33)
S = Single, **D** = Double/Twin, **T** = Triple, **Q** = Quad, **b** = bathroom, **s** = shower only, * = French hotel rating system (0-5 stars). Unless otherwise noted, credit cards are accepted, English is spoken, and prices do not include the city hotel tax.
To help you easily sort through these listings, I've divided the accommodations into three categories based on the price for a standard double room with bath:

$$$ Higher Priced—Most rooms €90 or more.
 $$ Moderately Priced—Most rooms between €60-90.
  $ Lower Priced—Most rooms €60 or less.

Prices can change without notice; verify the hotel's current rates online or by email. For the best prices, always book direct.

70 24 42, www.cardinal-hotel.fr, hotelcardinal.rouen@wanadoo.fr).

$$ Hôtel de la Cathédrale** welcomes you with a lovely courtyard and a cozy, wood-beamed breakfast room. Guest rooms are mostly country-French with basic bathrooms and imperfect sound insulation, but lots of character (Db-€90-120, Tb/Qb-€140-160, elevator, guest computer, Wi-Fi, 12 Rue St. Romain, a block from St. Maclou Church, tel. 02 35 71 57 95, www.hotel-de-la-cathedrale.fr, contact@hotel-de-la-cathedrale.fr).

$ Hôtel des Arcades is bare-bones basic, but as cheap and central as it gets (S-€42, D-€50 plus €5 to shower down the hall, Db-€56-62, 52 Rue des Carmes, tel. 02 35 70 10 30, www.hotel-des-arcades.fr, hotel_des_arcades@yahoo.fr).

Eating in Rouen

You can eat well in Rouen at fair prices. Because you're in Normandy, *crêperies* abound. For a simple meal inside or out, prowl the places between the St. Maclou and St. Ouen churches (along Rues Martainville and Damiette), or the ever-so-hip Rue de l'Eau de Robec. Otherwise, try the recommendations below.

Near the Cathedral

Crêperie le St. Romain, between the cathedral and St. Maclou Church, is an excellent budget option. It's run by gentle Mr. Pegis, who serves filling €9 crêpes with small salads in a warm setting (lunch Tue-Sat, dinner Thu-Sat, closed Sun-Mon, 52 Rue St. Romain, tel. 02 35 88 90 36).

Dame Cakes is ideal if it's lunchtime or teatime and you need a Jane Austen fix. The decor is from another, more precious era, and the baked goods are out of this world (€12-15 salads and *plats*, garden terrace in back, Mon-Sat 11:00-18:00, closed Sun, 70 Rue St. Romain, tel. 02 35 07 49 31).

La Petite Bouffe is a colorful, cheery place with tall windows, a young vibe, and good prices (€20 three-course *menus*, closed Sun, 1 Rue des Boucheries St-Ouen, tel. 02 35 98 13 14).

At **Flunch** you'll find family-friendly, cheap, point-and-shoot, cafeteria-style meals in a fast-food setting (*menus* for about €10 include salad bar, main course, and drink; good kids' *menu*, open daily until 22:00, a block from cathedral at 66 Rue des Carmes, tel. 02 35 71 81 81).

On Place du Vieux Marché

A fun lineup of restaurants—where locals wouldn't be caught dead—faces Place du Vieux Marché, across from the Joan of Arc Church. **Le Maupassant** is one of many, with an outdoor terrace and three lively floors filled with orange leather booths (regional *menus*, lunch from €18, dinner from €30, daily, 39 Place du Vieux Marché, tel. 02 35 07 56 90).

Les Nymphéas is *le place* to do it up well in Rouen. Indoor and garden tables are carefully set for lovers of fine cuisine (€44 and €54 *menus*, closed Sun-Mon, just off Place du Vieux Marché at 7 Rue de la Pie, tel. 02 35 89 26 69).

Rouen Connections

Rouen is well served by trains from Paris, via Amiens to other points north, and via Caen to other destinations west and south.

From Rouen by Train to: Paris' Gare St. Lazare (nearly hourly, 1.5 hours), **Bayeux** (4/day, 2.5 hours, change in Caen; more trips possible via Paris' Gare St. Lazare, 4-5 hours), **Pontorson/Mont St-Michel** (2/day, 4 hours, change in Caen; more with change in Paris, 7 hours).

By Train and Bus to: Honfleur (6/day Mon-Sat, 3/day Sun, 1-hour train to Le Havre, then easy transfer to 30-minute bus over Normandy Bridge to Honfleur—Le Havre's bus and train stations are adjacent).

Honfleur

Gazing at its cozy harbor lined with skinny, soaring houses, it's easy to overlook the historic importance of Honfleur (ohn-flur). For more than a thousand years, sailors have enjoyed this port's ideal loca-  tion, where the Seine River greets the English Channel. William the Conqueror received supplies shipped from Honfleur. Samuel de Champlain sailed from here in 1608 to North America, where he discovered the St. Lawrence River and founded Quebec City. The town was also a favorite of 19th-century Impressionists who were captivated by Honfleur's unusual light—the result of its river-meets-sea setting. Eugène Boudin (boo-dahn) lived and painted in Honfleur, drawing Monet and other creative types from Paris. In some ways, modern art was born in the fine light of idyllic little Honfleur.

Honfleur escaped the bombs of World War II, and today offers a romantic port enclosed on three sides by sprawling outdoor cafés. Long eclipsed by the gargantuan port of Le Havre just across the Seine, Honfleur happily uses its past as a bar stool...and sits on it.

Orientation to Honfleur

Honfleur is popular—be ready for crowds on weekends and during summer. All of Honfleur's engaging streets and activities are within a short stroll of its old port (Vieux Bassin). The Seine River flows just east of the center, the hills of the Côte de Grâce form its western limit, and Rue de la République slices north-south through the center to the port. Honfleur has two can't-miss sights—the harbor and Ste. Catherine Church—and a handful of other intriguing monuments. But really, the town itself is its best sight.

Tourist Information
The TI is in the flashy glass public library *(Mediathèque)* on Quai le Paulmier, two blocks from Vieux Bassin toward Le Havre (July-Aug Mon-Sat 9:30-19:00, Sun 10:00-17:00; Sept-June Mon-Sat 9:30-12:30 & 14:00-18:30, Sun 10:00-12:30 & 14:00-17:00 except closed Sun afternoon Oct-Easter; free WCs inside, pay Internet access, tel. 02 31 89 23 30, www.ot-honfleur.fr). Here you can rent a €3.50 audioguide for a self-guided town walk, or pick up a town map, bus and train schedules, and find information on the D-Day beaches.

Museum Pass: The €10 museum pass, sold at the TI and participating museums, covers the Eugène Boudin Museum, Maisons Satie, and the Museums of Old Honfleur (Museum of the Navy and Museum of Ethnography and Norman Popular Art); it pays for itself with visits to the Boudin and Satie museums (www.musees-honfleur.fr).

NORMANDY

Arrival in Honfleur

By Bus: Get off at the small bus station *(gare routière)*, and confirm your departure at the helpful information counter. To reach the TI and old town, turn right as you exit the station and walk five minutes up Quai le Paulmier. Note that the bus stop on Rue de la République may be more convenient for some accommodations.

By Car: Follow *Centre-Ville* signs, then find your hotel (easier said than done) and unload your bags (double-parking is OK for a few minutes). Parking is a headache in Honfleur, especially on summer and holiday weekends. Some hotels offer parking...for a price. Otherwise, your hotelier knows where you can park for free. The central Parking du Bassin (across from the TI) is pricey (€2/hour, €12/day). Across the short causeway is Parking du Môle, which is cheaper (only €4/day), but a bit less central. Parking Beaulieu is still farther (take Rue St-Nichol to Rue Guillaume de Beaulieu), but free. Street parking, metered during the day, is free from 20:00 to 8:00.

Helpful Hints

Market Day: The area around Ste. Catherine Church becomes a colorful open-air market every Saturday (9:00-13:00). A smaller organic-food-only market takes place here on Wednesday mornings, and a flea market takes center stage here the first Sunday of the month.

Grocery Stores: A good **Casino Grocery** is near the TI with long hours (daily July-Aug, closed Mon off-season, 16 Quai le Paulmier).

Regional Products with Panache: Visit **Produits Regionaux Gribouille** for any Norman delicacy you can dream up. Say *bonjour* to Monsieur Gribouille (gree-boo-ee) and watch your head—his egg-beater collection hangs from above (Thu-Tue 9:30-13:00 & 14:00-19:00, closed Wed, 16 Rue de l'Homme de Bois, tel. 02 31 89 29 54).

Internet Access: Free Wi-Fi is available at the relaxed **Travel Coffee Shop** (near the recommended La Cour Ste. Catherine B&B). The TI has a list of cafés with computer terminals and Wi-Fi.

NORMANDY

Honfleur

R. ALPHONESE ALLAIS
R. BAUDELAIRE
RUE DU TROILIMARD
RUE HAUTE
D-513
Jardin
BLVD. CHARLES V

MAISONS SATIE

CHARRIERE DE GRACE
R. L. DELARUE-MARDRUS
RUE DE L'HOMME DE BOIS

One-way streets →

RUE VARIN
RUE ALBERT I
RUE BOULANGER

EUGÈNE BOUDIN MUSEUM

200 Meters
200 Yards

RUE BUCAILLE
RUE JEAN DOUBLET
RUE CAPUCINS
RUE DES CAPUCINS
RUE BARBEL
RUE DES LINGOTS

To Côte de Grâce ←

CHARRIERE DE LA CROIX ROUGE

RUE DU PUITS

Place du Puits

RUE EUGÈNE BOUDIN
RUE BRULEE

RUE DE LA FOULERIE

RUE DES PRES

RUE DE LA REPUBLIQUE

Leaving Honfleur
(B)
(B) To Honfleur Center

To Free Parking Beaulieu

D-579A

---

1 Hôtel le Cheval Blanc
2 L'Absinthe Hôtel & Le Bouilland Normand Restaurant
3 Hôtel de l'Ecrin
4 Hôtel du Dauphin
5 Hôtel des Loges
6 Hôtel Monet
7 Ibis Budget Hotel
8 La Cour Ste. Catherine & Travel Coffee Shop
9 Le Fond de la Cour
10 Madame Bellegarde's Rooms
11 Côté Resto
12 Le Bréard Restaurant
13 Au P'tit Mareyeur Rest.

14 L'Homme de Bois Rest.
15 La Commanderie Rest.
16 Le Gambetta Rest.
17 Café de l'Hôtel de Ville
18 Waterfront Crêpe Stand
19 Le Marin, Le Perroquet Vert & L'Albatross Bars
20 Le Vintage Bar/Café
21 Casino Grocery
22 Produits Regionaux Gribouille
23 Launderette
24 Tourist Train Stop
25 Art Gallery Row
26 Jolie France Boat Tours
27 Calypso Boat Tours

NORMANDY

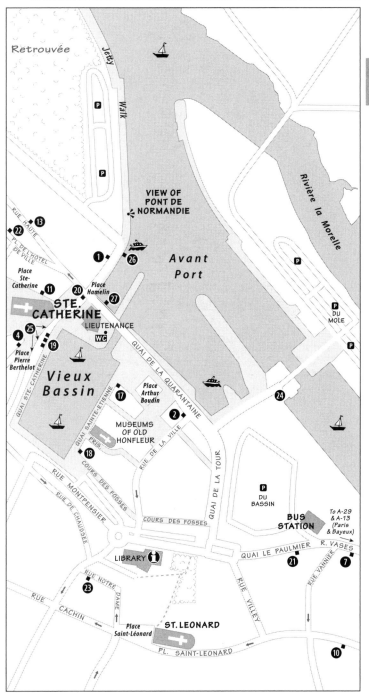

Retrouvée

Jetty Walk

View of Pont de Normandie

Avant Port

Rivière la Morelle

RUE HAUTE

PL. DE L'HÔTEL DE VILLE

Place Ste-Catherine

STE. CATHERINE

Place Hamelin

LIEUTENANCE

WC

Place Pierre Berthelot

Vieux Bassin

QUAI STE-CATHERINE

QUAI DE LA QUARANTAINE

Place Arthur Boudin

QUAI SAINTE-ÉTIENNE PRIS

MUSEUMS OF OLD HONFLEUR

RUE DE LA VILLE

COURS DES FOSSES

RUE MONTPENSIER

RUE DE CHAUSSÉE

COURS DES FOSSES

QUAI DE LA TOUR

DU BASSIN

BUS STATION

To A-29 & A-13 (Paris & Bayeux)

LIBRARY

QUAI LE PAULMIER

R. VASES

RUE VANNIER

RUE NOTRE DAME

RUE CACHIN

Place Saint-Léonard

ST. LEONARD

RUE VILLEY

PL. SAINT-LEONARD

Laundry: Lavomatique is a block behind the TI, toward the port (daily 7:30-20:00, 4 Rue Notre-Dame).

Taxi: Call mobile 06 18 18 38 38.

Tourist Train: Honfleur's *petit train* toots you up the Côte de Grâce—the hill overlooking the town—and back in about 50 minutes (€6.50, daily, departs from across gray swivel bridge that leads to Parking du Môle).

Sights in Honfleur

Vieux Bassin

Stand near the water facing Honfleur's square harbor, with the merry-go-round across the lock to your left, and survey the town.

The word "Honfleur" is Scandinavian, meaning the shelter *(fleur)* of Hon (a Norse settler). This town has been sheltering residents for about a thousand years. During the Hundred Years' War (14th century), the harbor was fortified by a big wall with twin gatehouses (the one surviving gatehouse, La Lieutenance, is on your right) and a narrow boat passage protected by a chain.

Those skinny houses on the right side were designed at a time when buildings were taxed based on their width, not height (and when knee replacements were unheard of). How about a room on the top floor, with no elevator? Imagine moving a piano into one of these units today. The spire halfway up the left side of the port belongs to Honfleur's oldest church and is now home to the Marine Museum. The port, once crammed with fishing boats, now harbors sleek sailboats. Walk toward the La Lieutenance gatehouse. In front of the barrel-vaulted arch (once the entry to the town), you can see a bronze bust of Samuel de Champlain—the explorer who sailed with an Honfleur crew 400 years ago to make his discoveries in Canada.

Turn around to see various tour and fishing boats and the high-flying Normandy Bridge (described later, under "Near Honfleur") in the distance. Fisherfolk catch flatfish, scallops, and tiny shrimp daily and bring them here. On the left you may see fishermen's wives selling *crevettes* (shrimp). You can buy them *cuites* (cooked) or *vivantes* (alive and wiggly). They are happy to let you sample one (rip off the cute little head and tail, and pop the middle into your mouth—*délicieuse!*), or buy a cupful to go for a few euros (daily in season).

You'll probably see artists sitting at easels around the harbor, as Boudin and Monet did. Many consider Honfleur the birthplace of 19th-century Impressionism. This was a time when people began to revere, not fear, the out-of-doors, and started to climb mountains "because they were there." Pretty towns like Honfleur and the nearby coast made perfect subjects to paint—and still are—thanks to what locals called the "unusual luminosity" of the region. And with the advent of trains in the late 1800s, artists could travel to the best light like never before. Artists would set up easels along the harbor to catch the light playing on the line of buildings, slates, timbers, geraniums, clouds, and reflections in the water. Monet came here to visit the artist Boudin, a hometown boy, and the battle cry of the Impressionists—"Out of the studio and into the light!"—was born.

If you're an early riser, you can watch what's left of Honfleur's fishing fleet prepare for the day, and you just might experience that famous luminosity.

▲▲Ste. Catherine Church (Eglise Ste. Catherine)
The unusual wood-shingled exterior suggests that this church has a different story to tell than most. Walk inside. You'd swear that if it were turned over, it would float—the legacy of a community of sailors and fishermen, with plenty of boat-builders and no cathedral architects. When workers put up the first nave in 1466, it soon became apparent that more space was needed—so the second was built in 1497. Because it felt too much like a market hall, they added side aisles. Notice the oak pillars, some full-length and others supported by stone bases. Trees come in different sizes, yet each pillar had to be the same thickness. In the last months of World War II, a bomb fell through the roof—but didn't explode. The pipe organ behind you is popular for concerts, and half of the modern pews are designed to flip so that you can face the music. Take a close look at the many medieval instruments carved into the railing below the organ—a 16th-century combo band in wood.

The church's bell tower is just as odd, because it was built not adjacent to the church but across the square. That's so it wouldn't overburden the wooden church's roof, and to help minimize fire hazards. Historians consider the structure ugly—I kind of like it. Notice the funky shingled beams that run from its squat base to support the skinny tower, and find the small, faded wooden sculpture of St. Catherine over the door. Peek inside to appreciate the ancient wood framing. The tiny museum, with a few church artifacts and a useful 15-minute video (in English) describes the tower's history.

Cost and Hours: Church—free, daily July-Aug 9:00-18:30, Sept-June 9:00-17:15; museum—not worth the entry fee but free with ticket to the Eugène Boudin Museum, April-Sept Wed-Mon 10:00-12:00 & 14:00-18:00; Oct-March Wed-Mon 14:00-18:00 only, closed Tue year-round.

Honfleur's Museums and Galleries

Remember, the €10 museum pass covers all four museums described below and pays for itself with visits to just the Boudin and Satie museums (pass sold at TI and participating museums).

▲Eugène Boudin Museum

This pleasing little museum has three interesting floors with many paintings of Honfleur and the surrounding countryside. The first floor displays Norman folk costumes, the second floor has the Boudin collection, and the third floor houses the Hambourg/Rachet collection and the Katia Granoff room.

Cost and Hours: €5.50, €2 extra during special exhibits, covered by museum pass, €2 English audioguide covers selected works (no English explanations on display—but none needed); mid-March-Sept Wed-Mon 10:00-12:00 & 14:00-18:00, closed Tue; Oct-mid-March Wed-Fri and Mon 14:30-17:30, Sat-Sun 10:00-12:00 & 14:30-17:30, closed Tue; elevator, no photos, Rue de l'Homme de Bois, tel. 02 31 89 54 00.

● **Self-Guided Tour:** Pick up a map at the ticket counter, tip your beret to Eugène Boudin, and climb the stairs (or take the elevator).

First Floor (Costumes): Monsieur and Madame Louveau (see their photo as you enter) gave Honfleur this quality collection of local traditional costumes. The hats, blouses, and shoes are supported by paintings that place them in an understandable historical and cultural context. Of special interest are the lace bonnets, typical of 19th-century Normandy. You could name a woman's village by her style of bonnet. The dolls are not toys for tots, but marketing tools for traveling clothing merchants—designed to show off the latest fashions. The men's department is in the back of the room.

Second Floor (Boudin Collection and More): Making a right off the stairs leads you into a large room of appealing 20th-century paintings and sculpture, created by artists who produced most of their works while living in Honfleur (special exhibits sometimes occupy this space). A left off the stairs leads through a temporary exhibition hall into the Salle Eugène Boudin, a small gallery of 19th-century paintings. In this room, Boudin's artwork is mixed with that of his colleagues and contemporaries; paintings by Claude Monet and Gustave Courbet are usually displayed. Find the glass display case in the rear titled *Précurseur de l'Impressionisme*, with little pastel drawings, and follow Boudin's art chronologically, as it evolves, from Romanticism through Realism to Impressionism (the heart of this museum).

Upon showing their work in Paris, local artists—such as Eugène Boudin—created enough of a stir that Normandy came into vogue; many Parisian artists (including Monet and other early Impressionists) traveled to Honfleur to dial in to the action. Boudin

Eugène Boudin (1824-1898)

Born in Honfleur, Boudin was the son of a harbor pilot. As an amateur teenage artist, he found work in an art-supply store that catered to famous artists from Paris (such as Jean-Baptiste-Camille Corot and Jean-François Millet) who came to paint the seaside. Boudin studied art in Paris but kept his hometown roots. Thanks to his Paris connections, Boudin's work was exhibited at the Paris salons.

At age 30 Boudin met the teenage Claude Monet. Monet had grown up in nearby Le Havre, and, like Boudin, sketched the world around him—beaches, boats, and small-town life. Boudin encouraged him to don a scarf, set up his easel outdoors, and paint the scene exactly as he saw it. Today, we say: "Well, duh!" But "open-air" painting was unorthodox for artists trained to thoroughly study their subjects in the perfect lighting of a controlled studio setting. Boudin didn't teach Monet as much as give him the courage to follow his artistic instincts.

In the 1860s and 1870s, Boudin spent summers at his farm (St. Siméon) on the outskirts of Honfleur, hosting Monet, Edouard Manet, and other hangers-on. They taught Boudin the Impressionist techniques of using bright colors and building a subject with many individual brushstrokes. Boudin adapted those "strokes" to build subjects with "patches" of color. In 1874, Boudin joined the renegade Impressionists at their "revolutionary" exhibition in Paris.

himself made a big impression on the father of Impressionism by introducing Monet to the practice of painting outside. This collection of Boudin's paintings—which the artist gave to his hometown—shows how his technique developed, from realistic portrayals of subjects (outlines colored in, like a coloring book) to masses of colors catching light (Impressionism). Boudin's beach scenes, showing aristocrats taking a healthy saltwater dip, helped fuel that style. His skies were good enough to earn him the nickname "King of Skies."

Third Floor (Hambourg/Rachet Collection): Follow the steps that lead from the Boudin room to the small Hambourg/Rachet collection (and a smashing painting of Honfleur at twilight). In 1988, André Hambourg and his wife, Nicole Rachet, donated their art to this museum. The collection is enjoyably Impressionistic, but largely from the mid-20th century.

Third Floor (Salle Katia Granoff): Retrace your steps back to the main stairway to reach the other third-floor room, where you'll find a worthwhile collection of 20th-century works by artists who lived and learned in Honfleur. Find the few paintings by Raoul Dufy (a French Fauvist painter) and compare his imaginative scenes of Normandy with others you've seen. Don't miss the brilliant view of the Normandy Bridge through the windows.

Art Galleries

Eugène Boudin ignited Honfleur's artistic tradition, which still burns today. The town is a popular haunt of artists, many of whom display their works in Honfleur's many art galleries (the best ones are along the streets between Ste. Catherine Church and the port). As you walk around the town, take the time to enjoy today's art.

▲Maisons Satie

If Honfleur is over-the-top cute, this remarkable museum, housed in composer Erik Satie's birthplace, is a refreshing burst of witty charm—just like the musical genius it honors. As you wander from room to room with your included audioguide, infrared signals transmit bits of Satie's minimalist music, along with a first-person story (in English). As if you're living as an artist in 1920s Paris, you'll drift past winged pears, strangers in the window, and small girls with green eyes. (If you like what you hear...don't move; the infrared transmission is hypersensitive, and the soundtrack switches every few feet.)

The finale—performed by you—is the *Laboratory of Emotions* pedal-go-round, a self-propelled carousel where your feet create the music (be sure to pedal softly). For a relaxing break, enjoy the 12-minute movie (4/hour, French only) featuring modern dance springing from *Parade*, Satie's collaboration with Pablo Picasso and Jean Cocteau; the Dadaist *Relâche*; and other works. You'll even hear the boos and whistles that greeted these ballets' debuts.

Cost and Hours: €6, includes audioguide, covered by museum pass; May-Sept Wed-Mon 10:00-19:00, closed Tue; Oct-Dec and mid-Feb-April Wed-Mon 11:00-18:00, closed Tue; closed Jan-mid-Feb; last entry one hour before closing, 5-minute walk from harbor at 67 Boulevard Charles V, tel. 02 31 89 11 11, www.musees-honfleur.fr.

Museums of Old Honfleur

Two side-by-side folk museums combine to paint a picture of daily life in Honfleur during the time when its ships were king and the city had global significance. The curator creatively supports the artifacts with paintings, making the cultural context clearer. Both museums have booklets with English explanations.

The **Museum of the Navy** (Musée de la Marine) faces the port and fills Honfleur's oldest church (15th century) with a cool collection of ship models, marine paraphernalia, and paintings. The **Museum of Ethnography and Norman Popular Art** (Musée d'Ethnographie et d'Art Populaire), located in the old prison and courthouse, re-creates typical rooms from various eras and crams them with objects of daily life (€3.80 each or €5 for both, covered by museum pass; both museums open April-Sept Tue-Sun 10:00-

12:00 & 14:00-18:30, closed Mon; March and Oct-Nov Tue-Fri 10:00-12:00 & 14:30-17:30, Sat-Sun 10:00-12:00 & 14:00-17:30, closed Mon; closed Dec-Feb).

Walks

▲Côte de Grâce Walk

For good exercise and a bird's-eye view of Honfleur and the Normandy Bridge, take the steep 20-minute walk (or quick drive) up to the Côte de Grâce viewpoint—best in the early morning or at sunset. From Ste. Catherine Church, walk or drive up Rue du Puits, then follow the blue-on-white signs to reach the splendid view. *Piétons* (walkers) should veer right up La Rampe du Mont Joli; *conducteurs* (drivers) should keep straight. Two hundred yards past the top, the **Chapel of Notre-Dame de Grâce** merits a visit. Built in the early 1600s by the mariners and people of Honfleur, the church oozes seafaring mementos. Model boats hang from the ceiling, pictures of boats balance high on the walls, and what's left is decorated by stained-glass images of sailors praying to the Virgin Mary while at sea. Even the holy water basins to the left and right of the entrance are in the shape of seashells. Try ringing the church bells hanging in the rack just outside.

Just below the chapel, a second lookout offers a sweeping view of super-industrial Le Havre, with·the Manche (English Channel) to your left and the Normandy Bridge to your right.

Jetty/Park Walk

Take a level stroll in Honfleur along the water past the Hôtel le Cheval Blanc to find the mouth of the Seine River and big ships at sea. You'll pass kid-friendly parks carpeted with flowers and grass, and continue past the lock connecting Honfleur to the Seine and the sea. Grand and breezy vistas of the sea reward the diligent walker (allow an hour round-trip for best views).

Near Honfleur

Boat Excursions

Boat trips in and around Honfleur depart near Hôtel le Cheval Blanc (Easter-Oct usually about 11:00-17:00). The tour boat *Calypso* takes good 45-minute spins around Honfleur's harbor (€6, mobile 06 71 64 50 46). The *Jolie France* cruises to the Normandy Bridge (see next), which, unfortunately, means two boring trips through the locks (€9.50/1.5 hours, mobile 06 71 64 50 46).

▲Normandy Bridge (Pont de Normandie)

The 1.25-mile-long Normandie Bridge is the longest cable-stayed bridge in the Western world (about €5 toll each way). This is a key piece of a super-expressway that links the Atlantic ports from Belgium to Spain. View the bridge from Honfleur (better from an excursion boat or the Côte de Grâce viewpoint, and best at night, when bridge is floodlit). Also consider visiting the bridge's free Exhibition Hall (under tollbooth on Le Havre side, daily 8:00-19:00). The Seine finishes its winding 500-mile journey here, dropping only 1,500 feet from its source. The river flows so slowly that, in certain places, a stiff breeze can send it flowing upstream.

▲Etrétat

France's answer to the White Cliffs of Dover, these chalky cliffs soar high above a calm, crescent beach (from Honfleur, it's about 50 minutes by car or 2 hours by bus via Le Havre). Walking trails lead hikers from the small seaside resort of Etrétat along a vertiginous route with sensational views (and crowds of hikers in summers and on weekends). You'll recognize these cliffs—and the arches and stone spire that decorate them—from countless Impressionist paintings, including several at the Eugène Boudin Museum in Honfleur. The small, Coney Island-like town holds plenty of cafés and a **TI** (Place Maurice Guillard, tel. 02 35 27 05 21, www.etretat.net).

Getting There: Etrétat is north of Le Havre. To get here by car, cross the Normandy Bridge and follow A-29, then exit at *sortie Etrétat.* Buses serve Etrétat from Le Havre's *gare routière,* adjacent to the train station (5/day, 1 hour, www.keolis-seine-maritime.com).

Sleeping in Etrétat: **$$$ Hôtel Dormy** makes a nice splurge if the scenery moves you (Db-€138-165, Route du Havre at the edge of Etrétat, tel. 02 35 27 07 88, www.dormy-house.com, info@etretat-hotel.com).

Sleeping in Honfleur

Though Honfleur is popular in summer, it's busiest on weekends and holidays when prices can rise (blame Paris). English is widely spoken (Honfleur is a popular weekend getaway for Brits). A few moderate accommodations remain, but most hotels are pretty pricey. Budget travelers should consider the *chambres d'hôtes* listed.

Only two hotels have elevators (Hôtel le Cheval Blanc and Ibis Budget Honfleur), but Hotel Monet has ground-floor units.

Hotels

$$$ Hôtel le Cheval Blanc*,** a Best Western, is a waterfront splurge with port views from all of its 35 plush and pricey rooms (many with queen-size beds), plus a rare-in-this-town elevator and a spa, but no air-conditioning—noise can be a problem with windows open (small Db with lesser view-€150, Db with full port view-€180-230, family rooms/suites-€280-435, must cancel by 16:00 the day before or forfeit deposit, free Wi-Fi, 2 Quai des Passagers, tel. 02 31 81 65 00, www.hotel-honfleur.com, info@hotel-honfleur.com).

$$$ L'Absinthe Hôtel*** offers 11 tastefully restored rooms, all with king-size beds. Rooms in the "old" section come with wood-beamed decor and Jacuzzi tubs, and share a cozy public lounge with a fireplace (Db-€160-210). Five rooms have port views and four-star, state-of-the-art comfort, including air-conditioning and saunas (Db-€170-190, Db suite-€265; breakfast-€13, private parking-€12, 1 Rue de la Ville, tel. 02 31 89 23 23, www.absinthe. fr, reservation@absinthe.fr).

$$$ Hôtel de l'Ecrin*** is a true Old World refuge. Enter the private courtyard to find a vintage mansion with lovely gardens and ample grass, a big pool, a sauna, public spaces Eugène Boudin would appreciate, free on-site parking, and *très* traditional rooms— some have four-poster *grand lits* (Db-€120, bigger Db-€145-155, big suites-€200-250, Wi-Fi, 10 minutes by foot from the harbor at 19 Rue Eugène Boudin, tel. 02 31 14 43 45, www.honfleur.com, hotel.ecrin@honfleur.com).

$$$ Hôtel du Dauphin** is centrally located, with a colorful lounge/breakfast room, many narrow stairs (normal in Honfleur),

and an Escher-esque floor plan. The 30 mostly smallish rooms—some with open-beam ceilings, some with queen- or king-size beds— provide reasonable comfort. If you need a lower floor or bigger bed, re-quest it when you book (Db-€100-125, Tb-€125-155, lovely Qb-€165, Wi-Fi in lobby, a stone's throw from Ste. Catherine Church at 10 Place Pierre Berthelot, tel. 02 31 89 15 53, www.hoteldudauphin. com, info@hoteldudauphin.com). The same owners also run the **$$$ Hôtel des Loges*****, a few doors up, which offers larger rooms with Wi-Fi, but less personality (Db-€115-140). Both hotels offer a 10 percent discount for Rick Steves readers in 2014 if you book direct—mention when you reserve and show this book at check-in.

$$ Hôtel Monet**, on the road to the Côte de Grâce and a 10-minute walk down to the port (longer back up), is an overlooked find. This tranquil spot is an ivy-covered brick home with 16 mostly tight but good-value rooms facing a courtyard, many with a patio made for picnics. You'll meet welcoming owners Christoph and Sylvie (Db-€64-104, Tb-€80-115, Qb-€92-150, highest rates are for July-Sept, free and easy parking, Wi-Fi, Charrière du Puits, tel. 02 31 89 00 90, www.hotel-monet.fr, contact@hotel-monet-honfleur.com).

$ Ibis Budget Honfleur is modern, efficient, trim, and cheap, with prefab bathrooms and an antiseptically clean ambience (Sb/Db/Tb-€59, cheaper off-season, reception is closed 21:00-6:00 but automatic check-in with credit card available 24 hours, elevator, free Wi-Fi, across from bus station and main parking lot on Rue des Vases, tel. 08 92 68 07 81, www.ibisbudget.com, h2716-re@accor.com).

Chambres d'Hôtes

The TI has a long list of Honfleur's many *chambres d'hôtes* (rooms in private homes), but most are too far from the town center. The three listed here are good values.

$$$ Le Fond de la Cour is where British expats Amanda and Craig offer a good mix of accommodations, including a large cottage that can sleep six, three apartments with small kitchens (Db-€85-130, extra person-€30, short stays possible), and two attractive B&B rooms (Db-€85-100, Tb-€130, includes English-style breakfast, Wi-Fi, free street parking, private parking-€9/day, 29 Rue Eugène Boudin, tel. 09 62 31 24 30, mobile 06 72 20 72 98, www.lefonddelacour.com, amanda.ferguson@orange.fr).

$$ La Cour Ste. Catherine, kitty-corner to Le Fond de la Cour, is an enchanting bed-and-breakfast run by the open-hearted Madame Giaglis ("call me Liliane") and her big-hearted husband, Monsieur Liliane. Her six big, modern rooms—each with firm beds and a separate sitting area—surround a perfectly Norman courtyard with a small terrace, fine plantings, and a cozy lounge area ideal for cool evenings. The rooms are as cheery as the owner—ask about her coffee shop (Db-€90, Db suite-€110, Tb/Qb-€150, extra bed-€30, includes breakfast, small apartments that sleep up to 6 and cottage with kitchen also available, cash only, guest computer, free Wi-Fi, free parking in 2014 with this book, 200 yards up Rue du Puits from Ste. Catherine Church at #74, tel. 02 31 89 42 40, www.coursaintecatherine.com, coursaintecatherine@orange.fr).

$ Sweet **Madame Bellegarde** offers two simple rooms in her traditional home (Db-€52-57, family-friendly Tb with great view from bathroom-€65, includes breakfast, cash only, 10-minute uphill walk from TI, 3 blocks up from St. Léonard Church in untouristy part of Honfleur, 54 Rue St. Léonard, look for small *chambres* sign in window, she'll try to hold a parking spot if you ask, tel. 02 31 89 06 52).

Eating in Honfleur

Eat seafood or cream sauces here. It's a tough choice between the irresistible waterfront tables of the many look-alike places lining the harbor and the eateries with more solid reputations elsewhere in town. Trust my dinner suggestions and consider your hotelier's opinion. It's best to call ahead to reserve at most restaurants in Honfleur (particularly on weekends).

Le Bouilland Normand hides a block off the port on a pleasing square and offers a true Norman experience at reasonable prices. Claire and Bruno provide quality *Normand* cuisine and enjoy helping travelers. Daily specials complement the classic offerings (€19.50-28 *menus,* closed Wed, dine inside or out, on Rue de la Ville, tel. 02 31 89 02 41, www.aubouillonnormand.fr).

Côté Resto saddles up on the left side of Ste. Catherine Church and serves a top selection of seafood (including seafood *choucroute* and real cheesecake—not served together) in a classy setting. The value is excellent for those in search of a special meal (€23 two-course *menu*, €28 three-course *menu*, great selection, closed Thu, 8 Place Ste. Catherine, tel. 02 31 89 31 33, www.cote-resto-honfleur.com).

Le Bréard serves exquisite modern French cuisine presented with care, style, and ingenuity. Book ahead, then savor a delicious, slow meal in a formal yet appealing setting—all for a fraction of the price you'd pay in Paris (€29, €45, and €55 *menus,* but only higher-priced *menus* Fri-Sat, closed Mon-Tue, 7 Rue du Puits, tel. 02 31 89 53 40, www.restaurant-lebreard.com).

Au P'tit Mareyeur is whisper-formal, intimate, all about seafood, and a good value. Reservations are particularly smart here (€35 four-course *menu,* closed Tue-Wed and Jan, 4 Rue Haute, tel. 02 31 98 84 23, mobile 06 84 33 24 03, www.auptitmareyeur.fr, friendly owner Julie speaks some English).

L'Homme de Bois combines great ambience with authentic Norman cuisine and decent prices (€21 three-course *menu* with few choices, €24 *menu* gives more choices, daily, a few outside tables, 30 Rue de l'Homme de Bois, tel. 02 31 89 75 27).

La Commanderie, specializing in pizza and crêpes (€10-12), is cozy and welcoming (daily July-Aug, closed Mon-Tue off-season, across from Le Corsaire restaurant on Place Ste. Catherine, tel. 02 31 89 14 92).

Le Gambetta is a good place whose sincere owners limit the selection in order to preserve the freshness of their products—it's a different set of options every day (€24 *menus,* closed Mon-Tue, 58 Rue Haute, tel. 02 31 87 05 01).

Travel Coffee Shop is an ideal breakfast or lunch option for travelers wanting conversation (in either English or French) and good food at very fair prices (Thu-Tue 8:00-19:00, closed Wed, 74 Rue du Puits).

Dining along the Harbor: If the weather cooperates, slide down to the harbor and table-shop the joints that line the high side. Several places have effective propane heaters that keep outdoor diners happy when it's cool. Although the cuisine is mostly mediocre, the setting is uniquely Honfleur—and, on a languid evening, hard to pass up. Take a stroll along the port and compare restaurant views, chair comfort, and menu selection (all of these places look the same to me). Then dive in and remember that you're paying for the setting, not the cuisine: Stick with basic dishes such as crêpes, omelets, pizza, or pasta. If you decide to eat elsewhere, at least come here for a before- or after-dinner drink—see "Nightlife," below.

Of the harbor-front options, **Café de l'Hôtel de Ville** owns the best afternoon sun exposure (and charges for it) and looks across to Honfleur's soaring homes (open daily July-Aug, closed Tue off-season, Place de l'Hôtel de Ville, tel. 02 31 89 07 29).

Breakfast: If it's even close to sunny, skip your hotel breakfast and enjoy ambience for a cheaper price by eating on the port, where several cafés offer *petit déjeuner* (€3-7 for continental fare, €7-13 for more elaborate choices). Morning sun and views are best from the high side of the harbor. If price or companionship matter, head to the Travel Coffee Shop for the best breakfast deal in town (described earlier).

Dessert: Honfleur is ice-cream crazy, with gelato and traditional ice cream shops on every corner. If you need a Ben & Jerry's ice cream fix or a scrumptious dessert crêpe, find the **waterfront stand** at the southeast corner of Vieux Bassin.

Nighttime Food to Go: Order a tasty pizza to go until late from **Il Parasole** (2 Rue Haute, tel. 02 31 98 94 29), and enjoy a picnic dinner with port views a few steps away in front of the La Lieutenance gatehouse.

Nightlife: Nightlife in Honfleur centers on the old port. Three bar/cafés sit almost side by side, halfway up the high-building side of the port. All offer waterfront tables if all you want is a drink: **Le Marin** (average), **L'Albatross** (pub-like with flags, banners, and a loyal following), and **Le Perroquet Vert** (existential—"those lights are so...").

Le Vintage, just off the port, is a happening bar/café with live piano and jazz on weekend nights. Casual outdoor seating and a vigorous interior make this a fun choice (closed Tue, 8 Quai des Passagers, tel. 02 31 89 05 28).

Honfleur Connections

There's no direct train service to Honfleur. The fastest and easiest way to connect to trains is to take the PrestoBus express—line #39—to Caen or Le Havre, but be aware that it runs only two or three times a day. Two slower bus routes connect Honfleur with Le Havre, Caen, Deauville, and Lisieux—all with direct rail service to Paris. Bus #50 runs between Le Havre, Honfleur and Lisieux;

bus #20 connects Le Havre, Honfleur, Deauville, and Caen. Although train and bus service usually are coordinated, confirm your connection with the helpful staff at Honfleur's bus station (English information desk open Mon-Fri 9:30-12:00 & 13:00-18:00, in summer also Sat-Sun, tel. 02 31 89 28 41, www.busverts.fr). If the station is closed, you can get schedules at the TI. Railpassholders will save money by connecting through Deauville, as bus fares increase with distance (Deauville to Honfleur-€2.30, Lisieux to Honfleur-€4.50).

From Honfleur by Bus and/or Train to: Caen (express buses 2-3/day, 1 hour; more scenic *par la côte* 4/day direct, 2 hours); **Bayeux** (6-7/day, 1.5-3 hours; options are 1-hour express bus or 2-hour bus via the coast to Caen, then 20-minute train to Bayeux); **Rouen** (6/day Mon-Sat, 3/day Sun, bus-and-train combo involves 30-minute bus ride over Normandy Bridge to Le Havre, then easy transfer to 1-hour train to Rouen); **Paris'** Gare St. Lazare (13/day, 2.5-3.5 hours, by bus to Caen, Lisieux, Deauville, or Le Havre, then train to Paris; buses from Honfleur meet most Paris trains).

Bayeux

Only six miles from the D-Day beaches, Bayeux was the first city liberated after the landing. Incredibly, the town was spared the bombs of World War II. After a local chaplain made sure London knew that his city was not a German headquarters and was of no strategic importance, a scheduled bombing raid was canceled—making Bayeux the closest city to the D-Day landing site not destroyed. Even without its famous medieval tapestry and proximity to the D-Day beaches, Bayeux would be worth a visit for its enjoyable town center and awe-inspiring cathedral, beautifully illuminated at night. Bayeux makes an ideal home base for visiting the area's sights, particularly if you lack a car.

Orientation to Bayeux

Tourist Information
The TI is on a small bridge two blocks north of the cathedral. Ask for the free *Exploration and Emotion: The Historical Area of the Battle of Normandy* booklet, bus schedules to the beaches, and regional information, and inquire about special events and concerts (TI open July-Aug Mon-Sat 9:00-19:00, Sun 9:00-13:00 & 14:00-18:00; Sept-June, Mon-Sat 9:30-12:30 & 14:00-18:00, Sun 10:00-13:00 & 14:00-18:00, on Pont St. Jean leading to Rue St. Jean, tel. 02 31 51 28 28, www.bessin-normandie.com).

NORMANDY

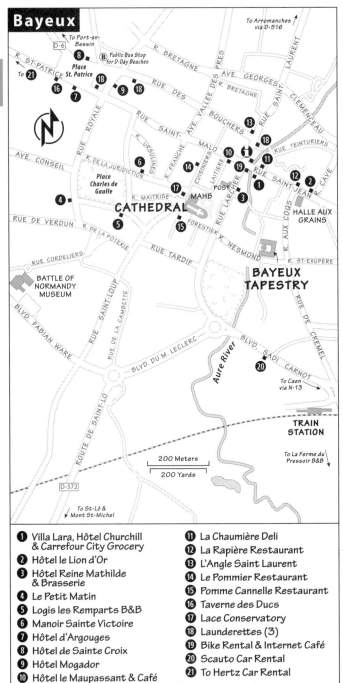

Bayeux

1 Villa Lara, Hôtel Churchill
& Carrefour City Grocery
2 Hôtel le Lion d'Or
3 Hôtel Reine Mathilde
& Brasserie
4 Le Petit Matin
5 Logis les Remparts B&B
6 Manoir Sainte Victoire
7 Hôtel d'Argouges
8 Hôtel de Sainte Croix
9 Hôtel Mogador
10 Hôtel le Maupassant & Café
11 La Chaumière Deli
12 La Rapière Restaurant
13 L'Angle Saint Laurent
14 Le Pommier Restaurant
15 Pomme Cannelle Restaurant
16 Taverne des Ducs
17 Lace Conservatory
18 Launderettes (3)
19 Bike Rental & Internet Café
20 Scauto Car Rental
21 To Hertz Car Rental

For a **self-guided walking tour,** pick up the map called *Découvrez Vieux Bayeux* at the TI. Follow the bronze plates embedded in the sidewalk, and look for information plaques with English translations that correspond to your map.

Museum Pass: Bayeux's three main museums—the Bayeux Tapestry, Battle of Normandy Memorial Museum, and MAHB—offer combo-tickets that will save you money if you plan to see more than one sight. Combo-tickets covering two sights cost €12; for all three it's €15 (buy it at the first sight you visit).

Arrival in Bayeux

By Train and Bus: Trains and buses share the same station (no bag storage). It's a 15-minute walk from the station to the tapestry, and 15 minutes from the tapestry to Place St. Patrice (and several recommended hotels). To reach the tapestry, the cathedral, and the hotels, cross the major street in front of the station and follow Rue de Cremel toward *l'Hôpital*, then turn left on Rue Nesmond. Find signs to the *Tapisserie* or continue on to the cathedral. Taxis are usually waiting at the station. Allow €8 for a taxi from the train station to any recommended hotel or sight in Bayeux, and €20 to Arromanches (€30 after 19:00 and on Sundays, taxi tel. 02 31 92 92 40 or mobile 06 70 40 07 96).

By Car: Look for the cathedral spires and follow signs for *Centre-Ville,* and then signs for the *Tapisserie* (tapestry) or your hotel (individual hotels are well-signed from the ring road—wait for yours to appear). Drivers connecting Bayeux with Mont St-Michel should use the speedy and free A-84 autoroute (closest entrance/exit for Bayeux is at Villers-Bocage; from Bayeux to A-84, take the underpass by the train station to Tilly-sur-Seulles, then Villers-Bocage).

Helpful Hints

Market Days: The Saturday open-air market on Place St. Patrice is Bayeux's best, though the Wednesday market on pedestrian Rue St. Jean is pleasant. Both end by 13:00. Don't leave your car on Place St. Patrice on a Friday night, as it will be towed early Saturday.

Grocery Store: Carrefour City, at Rue St. Jean 14, is next to the recommended Hôtel Churchill (Mon-Sat 7:00-22:00, Sun 9:00-13:00).

Internet Access: Right across from the TI, the souvenir shop **Aure Commun** has computer terminals and is open long hours (daily 9:00-20:00, shorter hours off-season, tel. 02 31 22 27 86). The recommended **La Reine Mathilde Brasserie** has free Wi-Fi for customers.

Laundry: A launderette with big machines is a block behind the

NORMANDY

TI, on Rue Maréchal Foch. Two more launderettes are near Place St. Patrice: One is at 4 Rue St. Patrice and the other is at 69 Rue des Bouchers (all open daily 7:00-21:00).

Bike Rental: Vélos Location has what you need and will deliver to outlying hotels (daily April-Oct 8:00-20:30, closes earlier off-season, across from the TI at Impasse de Islet, tel. 02 31 92 89 16).

Taxi: Call 02 31 92 92 40 or mobile 06 70 40 07 96.

Car Rental: Bayeux offers few choices. **Scauto** (at the Renault dealership) is handiest, just below the train station at the BP gas station. A rental at about €70/day with a 200-kilometer limit is sufficient to see the key sights from Arromanches to Utah Beach—you'll drive about 180 kilometers (16 Boulevard Sadi Carnot, tel. 02 31 51 18 51). **Hertz** is the only agency in town that allows you to drop off in a different city (located west of the city center on Route de Cherbourg, off D-613, tel. 02 31 92 03 26).

Day Trip to Caen Memorial Museum: France's most complete WWII museum is a manageable day trip from Bayeux, thanks to frequent and quick (20-minute) rail service between Bayeux and Caen, and easy access to the museum from Caen's train station. It's a 30-minute drive from Bayeux to the museum.

Sights in Bayeux

▲▲▲Bayeux Tapestry (Tapisserie de Bayeux)

Made of wool embroidered onto linen cloth, this historically precious document is a mesmerizing 70-yard-long cartoon. The tapestry tells the story of William the Conqueror's rise from duke of Normandy to king of England, and shows his victory over England's King Harold at the Battle of Hastings in 1066. Long and skinny, the tapestry was designed to hang in the nave of Bayeux's cathedral as a reminder for locals of their ancestor's courage. The  terrific museum that houses the tapestry is an unusually good chance to teach your kids about the Middle Ages: Models, mannequins, a movie, and more make it an engaging, fun place to visit.

Cost and Hours: €9, combo-ticket with other Bayeux museums €12 or €15, includes an excellent audioguide for adults and a special kids' version, daily May-Aug 9:00-18:15, March-April and Sept-Oct 9:00-17:45, Nov-Feb 9:30-11:45 & 14:00-17:15—these

Bayeux History—The Battle of Hastings

Because of this pivotal battle, the most memorable date of the Middle Ages is 1066. England's king, Edward the Confessor, was about to die without an heir. The big question: Who would succeed him—Harold, an English nobleman and the king's brother-in-law, or William, duke of Normandy and the king's cousin? Edward chose William, and sent Harold to Normandy to give William the news. On the journey, Harold was captured. To win his release, he promised he would be loyal to William and not contest the decision. To test his loyalty, William sent Harold to battle for him in Brittany. Harold was successful, and William knighted him. To further test his loyalty, William had Harold swear on the relics of the Bayeux cathedral that when Edward died, he would allow William to ascend the throne. Harold returned to England, Edward died...and Harold grabbed the throne.

William, known as William the Bastard, invaded England to claim the throne. Harold met him in southern England at the town of Hastings, where their forces fought a fierce 14-hour battle. Harold was killed, and his Saxon forces were routed. William—now "the Conqueror"—marched to London, claimed his throne, and became king of England (though he spoke no English) as well as duke of Normandy.

The advent of a Norman king of England muddied the political waters and set in motion 400 years of conflict between England and France—not to be resolved until the end of the Hundred Years' War (1453). The Norman conquest of England brought that country into the European mainstream (but still no euros). The Normans established a strong central English government. Historians speculate that had William not succeeded, England would have remained on the fringe of Europe (like Scandinavia), and French culture (and language) would have prevailed in the New World—which would have meant no communication issues for us in France. Hmmm.

are first and last entry times, tel. 02 31 51 25 50, www.tapisserie-bayeux.fr. To avoid crowds, arrive by 9:00 or late in the day.

Film: When buying your ticket, ask when they'll show the English version of the 15-minute battle film (runs every 40 minutes, English times also posted at the base of the steps to the theater).

Visiting the Museum: Your visit has three separate parts that tell the basic story of the Battle of Hastings, provide historical context for the event, and explain how the tapestry was made. At a minimum, allow a full hour to appreciate this important artifact.

Your visit starts with the actual **tapestry,** accompanied by an included audioguide that gives a top-notch, fast-moving, 20-minute scene-by-scene narration complete with period music (if you lose your place, find subtitles in Latin). Learn to pause your audioguide so you can stop and focus when and where you want. Pay attention to scene 23, where Harold reneges on his oath to William and takes the crown of England. Get close and (almost) feel the tapestry's texture.

Next you'll climb upstairs into a room filled with engaging exhibits, including a full-size replica of the boats William used to cross the Channel, mannequins (find William looking unmoved with his new crown), terrific models of castles (who knew that the Tower of London was a Norman project?), and medieval villages. Good explanations outline the events surrounding the invasion and the subsequent creation of the tapestry. Your visit finishes with a worthwhile 15-minute **film** that ties it all together one last time (in the cinema). You'll exit below, through a *formidable* boutique.

Remember, this is Norman propaganda—the English (the bad guys, referred to as *les goddamns,* after a phrase the French kept hearing them say) are shown with mustaches and long hair; the French (*les* good guys) are clean-cut and clean-shaven—with even the backs of their heads shaved for a better helmet fit.

▲▲Bayeux Cathedral
This massive building, as big as Paris' Notre-Dame, dominates the small town of Bayeux. (Make it a point to see the cathedral after dark, when it's beautifully illuminated.)

Cost and Hours: Free, daily July-Aug 8:30-19:00, Sept-June 8:30-18:00.

Visiting the Cathedral: To start your visit, find the small **square** opposite the front entry (information board about the cathedral in rear corner). Notice the two dark towers—originally Romanesque, they were capped later with tall Gothic spires. The cathedral's west facade is structurally Romanesque, but with a decorative Gothic "curtain" added.

Before entering, head just to the left of the cathedral and find the stairs at the top of a walking lane (another information panel is close by). The little rectangular stone house atop the near tower was the **watchman's home,** from which he'd keep an eye out for incoming English troops during the Hundred Years' War...and for Germans five centuries later (it didn't work—the Germans took the town in 1940). Bayeux was liberated on D-Day plus one: June 7. About the only casualty was the German lookout—shot while doing just that from the window of this stone house.

Now step inside the cathedral. The view of the **nave** from the top of the steps shows a mix of Romanesque and Gothic. Historians believe the Bayeux tapestry originally hung here. Imagine it proudly circling the Norman congregation, draped around the nave above the big arches. This section is brightly lit by the huge windows above, in the Gothic half of the nave. The glass was originally richly colored (see the rare surviving 13th-century bits in the high central window above the altar).

Walk down the nave and notice the areas between the big, round **arches.** That busy zigzag patterning characterizes Norman art in France as well as in England. These 11th-century Roman-esque arches are decorated with a manic mix of repeated geometric shapes: half-circles, interlocking hatch marks, full circles, and di-agonal lines. Notice also the creepy faces eyeing you, especially the ring of devil heads three arches up on the right. Yikes.

Information panels in the side aisles give basic facts about the cathedral (in English). More 13th-century Norman Gothic is in the choir (the fancy area behind the central altar). Here, simple Romanesque carvings lie under Gothic arches with characteristic tall, thin lines adding a graceful verticality to the overall feel of the interior.

For maximum 1066 atmosphere, step into the spooky **crypt** (beneath the central altar), which was used originally as a safe spot for the cathedral's relics. The crypt displays two freestanding columns and bulky capitals with fine Romanesque carving. Dur-ing a reinforcement of the nave, these two columns were replaced. Workers removed the Gothic veneer and discovered their true inner Romanesque beauty. Orange angel-musicians add color to this somber room.

River Walk

Join the locals and promenade along the meandering walking path that follows the little Aure River for about 2.5 miles through Bay-eux. The path runs both ways from the TI (find the waterwheel behind the TI and keep walking; path marked on city maps).

Lace Conservatory (Conservatoire de la Dentelle)

Notable for its carved 15th-century facade, the Adam and Eve house (find Adam, Eve, and the snake) offers a chance to watch workers design and weave intricate lace, just as artisans did in the 1600s. Enter to the clicking sound of the small wooden bobbins used by the lace-makers, and appreciate the concentration that their work requires. You can also see examples of lace from the past.

Cost and Hours: Free, Mon-Sat 9:30-12:30 & 14:30-18:00, until 17:00 Mon-Tue, closed Sun, across from cathedral entrance, tel. 02 31 92 73 80, http://dentelledebayeux.free.fr.

MAHB (Musée d'Art et d'Histoire Baron Gérard)

For a break from D-Day and tapestries, MAHB offers a modest review of European art and history in what was once the Bayeux bishop's palace. The core of the museum is a collection of 18th- and 19th-century paintings donated by Baron Henri-Alexandre Gérard more than a century ago. Notable are an early work by neoclassical master Jacques-Louis David—*Le Philosophe (The Phi-losopher)*—and *Sapho* by Antoine-Jean Gros, a moonlit version of the Greek poetess' death that influenced Géricault and Delacroix. Don't miss the museum's 19th-century courtroom and its elaborate chapel—gushing with early 17th-century "angels" that look like oversexed cherubs.

Cost and Hours: €7, combo-ticket with other Bayeux museums €12 or €15, daily May-Sept 9:30-12:30 & 14:00-18:30, shorter hours off-season, near the cathedral at 37 Rue du Bienvenu, tel. 02 31 92 14 21, www.bayeuxmuseum.com.

▲Battle of Normandy Memorial Museum (Musée Memorial de la Bataille de Normandie)

This museum provides a manageable overview of WWII's Battle of Normandy. With its many maps and timelines of the epic battle to liberate northern France, it's aimed at military history buffs—others may suffer from information overload. Still, it's worthwhile, especially if you won't be visiting Caen's Memorial Museum. You'll get a good briefing on the Atlantic Wall (the German fortifications stretching along the coast—useful before visiting Longues-sur-Mer), learn why Normandy was selected as the landing site, understand General Charles de Gaulle's contributions to the invasion, and realize the key role played by aviation. You'll also appreciate the challenges faced by doctors, war correspondents, and civil engineers (who had to clean up after the battles—the gargantuan bulldozer on display looks useful).

Cost and Hours: €7, combo-ticket with other Bayeux museums €12 or €15, daily May-Sept 9:30-18:30, Oct-Dec and mid-Feb-April 10:00-12:30 & 14:00-18:00, closed Jan-mid-Feb, on Bayeux's ring road, 20 minutes on foot from center on Boulevard Fabian Ware, tel. 02 31 51 46 90, www.normandiememoire.com.

Film: A 25-minute film gives a good summary of the Normandy invasion from start to finish (shown in English May-Sept at 10:30, 12:00, 14:00, 15:30, and 17:00; Oct-April at 10:30, 14:45, and 16:15).

Nearby: A right out of the museum leads along a footpath to the **Monument to Reporters,** a grassy walkway lined with white roses and stone monuments listing, by year, the names of reporters who have died in the line of duty from 1944 to today. Some years have been kinder to journalists than others. The path continues to the **British Military Cemetery,** decorated with 4,144 simple gravestones marking the final resting places of these fallen soldiers. The memorial's Latin inscription reads, "In 1944, the British came to free the homeland of William the Conqueror." Interestingly, this cemetery has soldiers' graves from all countries involved in the battle of Normandy (even Germany) except the United States, which requires its soldiers to be buried on US property—such as the American Cemetery at Omaha Beach.

Sleeping in Bayeux

Hotels are a good value here, and it's just a short hop from Bayeux to the D-Day beaches. Drivers should see "Sleeping near Omaha Beach" and "Sleeping in Arromanches" for more options.

Near the Tapestry

$$$ Villa Lara** owns the town's most luxurious accommodations smack in the center of Bayeux. The 28 spacious and well-configured rooms all have brilliant views of the cathedral, and a few have small terraces. The professional owners—the Héberts—and their well-trained staff take excellent care of their guests (Db-€220-280, Db suite-€350-450, elevator, Wi-Fi, exercise room, ice machines, comfortable lounges, free and secure parking, between the tapestry museum and TI at 6 Place de Québec, tel. 02 31 21 31 80, www.hotel-villalara.com, info@hotel-villalara.com).

$$$ Hôtel Churchill*,** on a traffic-free street across from the TI, could not be more central. Owners Eric and Patricia Pean are eager help you plan your time in their city (ask Eric about his professional soccer career, which included exhibition matches in the US). The hotel has 32 plush rooms with wood furnishings, big beds, and convivial public spaces peppered with historic photos of Bayeux's liberation (standard Db-€125, superior Db-€150, deluxe Db or Tb-€182, Qb-€202, Wi-Fi, 14 Rue St. Jean, tel. 02 31 21 31 80, www.hotel-churchill.fr, info@hotel-churchill.fr).

$$$ Hôtel le Lion d'Or*,** General Eisenhower's favorite hotel in Bayeux, draws an older clientele willing to pay top euro for its Old World character, professional service, and elegant restaurant. The place lives on its reputation, but could use a little work (standard Db-€125-135, bigger Db-€135-145, still bigger Db-€155-165, extra bed-€30, breakfast-€13, no elevator, Wi-Fi, easy parking-€9/day, 71 Rue St. Jean, tel. 02 31 92 06 90, www.liondor-bayeux.fr, info@liondor-bayeux.fr).

$$ Hôtel Reine Mathilde** is a solid, centrally located value with painless parking and good service. There are 16 tight but sharp rooms above an easygoing brasserie (Db-€60-85, Tb-€70-95, Qb-€85-100), and six larger rooms with three-star comfort next door (Db-€90-115, Tb-€100-125, breakfast-€8.50, Wi-Fi, one block from the TI at 23 Rue Larcher, tel. 02 31 92 08 13, www.hotel-bayeux-reinemathilde.fr, hotel.reinemathilde@orange.fr).

Chambres d'Hôtes near the Cathedral

$$$ Le Petit Matin, run by friendly Pascal, is a central, comfy, and traditional bed-and-breakfast that is well-located on Place

Charles de Gaulle (Db-€90-110, 9 Rue des Terres, tel. 02 31 10 09 27, www.lepetitmatin.com).

$$ Logis les Remparts is a delightful, three-room bed-and-breakfast run by charming Christèle and situated above an atmospheric Calvados cider-tasting shop. Rooms are big, comfortable, and homey—one is a huge, two-room suite (Db-€65-90, Tb-€80-100, Qb-€130, cash only for payments under €100, breakfast-€7, Wi-Fi downstairs in shop, a few blocks above the cathedral on the park-like Place Charles de Gaulle at 4 Rue Bourbesneur, tel. 02 31 92 50 40, www.lecornu.fr, info@lecornu.fr).

$$ Manoir Sainte Victoire is a classy, 17th-century building with three comfortable rooms, each dedicated to a different modern artist, and each with views of the cathedral (Db-€90, includes breakfast; rooms have small kitchenettes, Wi-Fi; 32 Rue de la Jurisdiction, tel. 02 31 22 74 69, mobile 06 37 36 90 95, www.manoirsaintevictoire.com, contact@manoirsaintevictoire.com).

Near Place St. Patrice

These hotels just off the big Place St. Patrice (easy parking) are a 10-minute walk up Rue St. Martin from the TI (a 15-minute walk to the tapestry).

$$$ Hôtel d'Argouges****** (dar-goo-zhah) makes an impression as you enter. Named for its builder, Lord d'Argouges, this tranquil retreat has a mini-château feel, with classy public spaces, lovely private gardens, and standard-comfort rooms. Its courtyard setting makes it quieter than many other Bayeux accommodations. The hotel is run by formal Madame Ropartz, who has had every aspect of the hotel renovated (Db-€136-155, Tb-€188, fine family suites-€240, deluxe mega-suite for up to 6 and good for two couples-€350, includes good breakfast, extra bed-€15, secure free parking, just off Place St. Patrice at 21 Rue St. Patrice, tel. 02 31 92 88 86, www.hotel-dargouges.com, info@hotel-dargouges.com).

$$ Hôtel de Sainte Croix offers three big rooms with cavernous bathrooms in a traditional manor home (Db-€89, Tb-€130, Qb-€160, cash only, includes good breakfast, 12 Rue du Marché at Place St. Patrice, mobile 06 08 09 62 69, www.hotel-de-sainte-croix.com, contact@hotel-de-sainte-croix.com, friendly Florence).

$$ Hôtel Mogador** is a good two-star value. Choose between simple, wood-beamed rooms on the busy square, or quiet but slightly faded rooms off the street. There are no public areas beyond the small breakfast room and tiny courtyard (Sb-€48-53, Db-€53-63, Tb-€71-74, Qb-€82-87, breakfast-€7.50, Wi-Fi, 20 Rue Alain Chartier at Place St. Patrice, tel. 02 31 92 24 58, www.hotelmo.fr, lemogador@gmail.com).

$ Hôtel le Maupassant offers 10 no-star, no-frills rooms with just enough comfort. The rooms are above a central café, and the bartender doubles as the receptionist (S-€38, D-€45, Db-€48, Ts-€75, Wi-Fi, 19 Rue St. Martin, tel. 02 31 92 28 53, h.lemaupassant@orange.fr).

In the Countryside near Bayeux

$$$ La Ferme du Pressoir is a lovely, traditional B&B on a big working farm that is immersed in Norman landscapes about 20 minutes south of Bayeux. If you've ever wanted to stay on a real French farm yet rest in cozy comfort, this is the place. The five rooms are filled with wood furnishings and decorated with bright garden themes. Guests share a kitchenette off the breakfast room; larger groups can stay in a cottage with its own kitchen. The experience is vintage Normandy—and so are the kind owners, Jacques and Odile, who communicate great warmth though they don't speak English (Db-€90, Tb-€110, Qb-€130, 5 people-€140, discounts for stays of 3 or more nights, includes good breakfast, tel. 02 41 40 71 07, Le Haut St-Louet, just off A-84, exit at Villers-Bocage, get detailed directions from website, www.bandbnormandie. com, lafermedupressoir@bandbnormandie.com).

Eating in Bayeux

Drivers can also consider the short drive to Arromanches for seaside options.

On or near Traffic-Free Rue St. Jean

This street is lined with cafés, *créperies,* and inexpensive dining options.

La Chaumière is the best charcuterie (deli) in town; you'll find salads, quiches, and prepared dishes to go (Tue-Sun open until 19:30, closed for lunch Sun and all day Mon, on Rue St. Jean across from Hôtel Churchill). The grocery store across the street has what you need to complete your picnic.

La Rapière is a lovely, traditional wood-beamed eatery filled with locals enjoying a refined meal and a rare-these-days cheese platter for your finale. The veal with Camembert sauce is memorable (€29-38 *menus,* closed Sun-Mon, 53 Rue St. Jean, tel. 03 31 21 05 45, www.larapiere.net).

L'Angle Saint Laurent is a popular bistro, run by a husband-and-wife team (lovely Caroline manages the restaurant, Sébastien cooks). You'll dine well on *Normand* specialties in a smart setting (€25-35 *menus,* closed Sun evening-Mon, 2 Rue des Bouchers, tel. 02 31 92 03 01).

La Reine Mathilde Brasserie, a service-oriented spot, offers bistro fare all day (omelets, big salads, pizza). It also has a marvelous outside terrace with cathedral views (daily with nonstop service 12:00-21:00, a block from Rue St. Jean at 23 Rue Larcher).

Near the Cathedral

Le Pommier, with street appeal both inside and out, is a good place to sample regional products with clever twists in a relaxed yet refined atmosphere. Owner Thierry mixes old and new in his cuisine and decor and focuses on organic food with no GMOs. His fish and meat dishes are satisfying no matter how he prepares them, and there's a vegetarian *menu* as well—a rarity in meat-loving France (good three-course *menu* from €24, open daily, 38 Rue des Cuisiniers, tel. 02 31 21 52 10).

Pomme Cannelle is cheap and easy, featuring crêpes, salads, and more for €9, inexpensive *menus*, and best—a killer view of the cathedral from the front terrace (open daily, 2 Impasse Prud'Homme, tel. 02 31 92 95 09).

On Place St. Patrice

Taverne des Ducs provides big brasserie ambience, efficient and friendly service with English-speaking staff, comfortable seating inside and out, a full range of choices from *la carte*—including French onion soup, *choucroute* (sauerkraut), and all the classics— and set *menus*. Try the cooked oysters with garlic sauce, or the *dos de cabillaud au beurre* (cod in butter sauce). They serve until 23:00 (*menus* from €19.50, open daily, 41 Rue St. Patrice, tel. 02 31 92 09 88).

Bayeux Connections

From Bayeux by Train to: Paris' Gare St. Lazare (9/day, 2.5 hours, some change in Caen), **Amboise** (3/day, 4.5 hours, change in Caen and Tours' St-Pierre-des-Corps), **Rouen** (4/day, 2.5 hours, change in Caen), **Caen** (20/day, 20 minutes), **Honfleur** (2-3/day, 20-minute train to Caen, then 1-hour PrestoBus—line #39—express bus to Honfleur; or 4/day 20-minute train to Caen and more scenic 2-hour ride on bus #20 via the coast; for bus information, call 02 31 89 28 41, www.busverts.fr), **Pontorson/Mont St-Michel** (2-3/day, 2 hours to Pontorson, then bus to Mont St-Michel; also consider Hôtel Churchill's faster shuttle van—described later).

By Bus to the D-Day Beaches: Bus Verts du Calvados offers minimal service to D-Day beaches with stops in Bayeux at Place St. Patrice and at the train station (schedules at TI, tel. 08 10 21 42 14, www.busverts.fr). Lines #74/#75 run east to Arromanches and Juno Beach (3-5/day, none on Sun Sept-June; 30 minutes to Arromanches, 50 minutes to Juno Beach), and line #70 runs west to the American Cemetery and Vierville-sur-Mer (3/day in summer, 1-2/ day off-season, none on Sun Sept-June, 35 minutes to American Cemetery, 45 minutes to Vierville-sur-Mer). Because of the schedules, you're usually stuck with either too much or too little time at either sight if you try to take the bus round-trip; consider a taxi one way and a bus the other.

By Shuttle Van to Mont St-Michel: The recommended **Hôtel Churchill** runs a shuttle van to Mont St-Michel for €65 per person round-trip (1.5 hours each way; available to the general public, though hotel clients get a small discount). The van leaves Bayeux at 8:30 and returns by 15:00, allowing travelers three hours at Mont St-Michel. The trip is a terrific deal as you'll get a free tour of Normandy along the way from your knowledgeable driver. For details, see www.hotel-churchill.fr.

D-Day Beaches

The 75 miles of Atlantic coast north of Bayeux, stretching from Ste-Marie-du-Mont to Ouistreham, are littered with WWII museums, monuments, cemeteries, and battle remains left in tribute to the courage of the British, Canadian, and American armies that successfully carried out the largest military operation in history: D-Day. (It's called *Jour J* in French—the letters "D" and "J" come from the first letter for the word "day" in either English or French.) It was on these serene beaches, at the crack of dawn on June 6, 1944, that the Allies finally gained a foothold in France, and Nazi Europe was doomed to crumble.

"The first 24 hours of the invasion will be decisive... The fate of Germany depends on the outcome... For the Allies, as well as Germany, it will be the longest day."
—Field Marshal Erwin Rommel to his aide, April 22, 1944 (from *The Longest Day,* by Cornelius Ryan)

June of 2014 marks the 70th anniversary of the landings. There will be huge D-Day commemorations around June 6—many heads of state are likely to attend, but there are only a few veterans still alive for these solemn ceremonies. (If you plan to come near the anniversary, you'll need to book about six months ahead.) All along this rambling coast, locals will never forget what the troops and their families sacrificed all those years ago. A warm regard for Americans has survived political disputes, from de Gaulle to "Freedom Fries." This remains particularly friendly soil for Americans—a place where their soldiers are still honored and the image of the US as a force for good has remained largely untarnished.

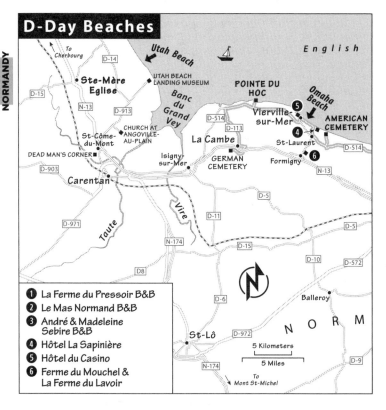

D-Day Beaches

To Cherbourg

D-14

Utah Beach

UTAH BEACH LANDING MUSEUM

English

POINTE DU HOC

Omaha Beach

Ste-Mère Eglise

D-15

N-13

D-913

Banc du Grand Vey

Vierville-sur-Mer

AMERICAN CEMETERY

D-514

CHURCH AT ANGOVILLE-AU-PLAIN

St-Côme-du-Mont

La Cambe

St-Laurent

D-113

DEAD MAN'S CORNER

Isigny-sur-Mer

GERMAN CEMETERY

Formigny

D-514

D-903

Carentan

N-13

D-971

Taute

Vire

D-5

D-11

D-5

N-174

D-15

D-10

D-572

D8

D-6

Balleroy

❶ La Ferme du Pressoir B&B
❷ Le Mas Normand B&B
❸ André & Madeleine Sebire B&B
❹ Hôtel La Sapinière
❺ Hôtel du Casino
❻ Ferme du Mouchel & La Ferme du Lavoir

St-Lô

D-972

N-174

NORM

5 Kilometers

5 Miles

D-9

To Mont St-Michel

Planning Your Time

I've listed the D-Day sites from east to west, starting with Arromanches (note that several are closed in January). Americans prefer to focus on the American sector (west of Arromanches), rather than the British and Canadian sectors (east of Arromanches), which have been overbuilt with resorts, making it harder to envision the events of June 1944. For more information on visiting the D-Day beaches, www.normandiememoire.com is a useful resource.

D-Day Sites in One Day

If you only have one day, I'd spend it entirely on the beaches and miss the Caen Memorial Museum. (If you want to squeeze in the museum, visit it on your way to or from the beaches—but remember that the American Cemetery closes at 18:00 mid-April–mid-Sept and at 17:00 the rest of the year—and you need at least 1.5 hours there.) With the exciting sites and museums along the beaches, the Caen Memorial Museum is less important for most.

If you're traveling **by car,** begin on the cliffs above Arromanches. Drive a quarter-mile downhill to the town and visit Port

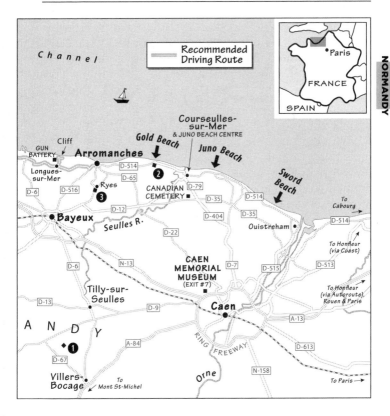

Winston and the D-Day Landing Museum, then continue west to Longues-sur-Mer. Spend your afternoon visiting the American Cemetery and its thought-provoking visitors center, walking on the beach at Vierville-sur-Mer, and exploring the Pointe du Hoc Ranger Monument. Try to find time for the terrific Utah Beach Landing Museum.

Other good options include visiting the strategic town of Ste-Mère Eglise to learn about the paratroopers' role in the invasion, and a quick stop at the German Military Cemetery. Canadians will want to start at the Juno Beach Centre and Canadian Cemetery (in Courseulles-sur-Mer, 10 minutes east of Arromanches), then pick up the itinerary described above.

For those **sans car,** it's easiest to take a minivan tour or taxi from Bayeux, or—for a really full day—combine a visit to the Caen Memorial Museum with their guided minivan tour of the beaches. Public transport is available, but not practical since it is very limited. Many find that a one-day car rental works best.

With More Time

Ideally, spend one day at Arromanches and the Omaha Beach sites, and another half-day at the Utah Beach sites (then head off to Mont St-Michel or Honfleur).

Getting Around the D-Day Beaches

On Your Own

Though the minivan excursions listed below teach important history lessons—drawing Americans and Canadians out of their cars—**renting a car** is a less expensive way to visit the beaches, particularly for three or more people.

However, if you're staying in Paris and want to make the D-Day beaches a day-trip in a rental car, think twice. A train from Paris to Caen (the most convenient place to pick up a car) takes over two hours. Then you'll face rental paperwork and at least a half-hour drive to your first stop at Arromanches. At a minimum, just getting to and from the D-Day beaches will take 6-7 hours out of your day—severely limiting your time at any one sight (many close at 18:00). A better alternative for Paris-based travelers is to book a service that will meet you at a train station and drive you to sights (see "By Taxi" and "By Fully Guided Minivan Tour" next). Or take a bus tour that starts in Paris.

Note that driving in France can be stressful for the average American unused to narrow roads, confusing signage, and tailgating French drivers. Park in monitored locations at the sites, since break-ins are a problem—particularly at the American Cemetery—and consider hiring a guide to enrich the experience—and help navigate (see "Private Tours," later).

Hardy souls can **bike** between some sites (though distances are long enough to discourage most). Very limited **bus service** links Bayeux, the coastal town of Arromanches, and the most impressive sites of D-Day. Consider a bus one way and taxi the other. For small groups, hiring a **taxi for the day** is far cheaper than taking a minivan tour, but you don't get the history.

By Taxi

Taxi minivans shuttle up to seven people between the key sites at reasonable rates (which vary depending on how far you go). Allow €240 for an eight-hour taxi day (€300 on Sun) to visit the top Utah and Omaha Beach sites. Figure about €21 each way between Bayeux and Arromanches, €36 between Bayeux and the American Cemetery, and €95 for a 2.5-hour visit to Omaha Beach sites from Bayeux or Arromanches (50 percent surcharge after 19:00 and on Sun, taxi tel. 02 31 92 92 40 or mobile 06 70 40 07 96, www.taxis-bayeux.com, taxisbayeux@orange.fr).

Abbeilles Taxis offer D-Day excursions from Caen (€130-3.5-hour visit to Omaha Beach sites, €270-full-day visit, tel. 02 31 52 17 89, www.taxis-abbeilles-caen.com).

By Fully Guided Minivan Tour

An army of small companies offers all-day excursions to the D-Day beaches from Bayeux or nearby. The tour companies and guides listed in this section are all quality operators that I trust. Most deliver riveting commentary about these moving sites. Because they pick up and drop off at select train stations, they are popular with day-trippers from Paris. To land one of these top-notch guides, book your tour as far in advance as possible (three months is best), or pray for a last-minute cancellation. The best

way to save on the cost is to hire a guide who offers half-day tours or one who is willing to join you in your rental car (noted in listings below).

Cost: These tours are pricey, because you're hiring a professional guide and driver/vehicle for the day. All guides charge about the same. A few have regularly scheduled departures available for individual sign-up (expect to pay about €50-60/person for a half-day and €90/person for a full day), but many take only private groups (figure €475-550 for up to eight people). Most tours don't go inside museums (which are self-explanatory), but those that do usually include entry fees—ask. Although many operators offer all-day tours only, these guides may do half-day trips: Paul de Winter, Normandy Sightseeing Tours, Vanessa Letourneur, Edward Robinson, Eva Ruttger, Victory Tours, and Mathias Leclere.

Working with Your Guide: Request extra time at the American Cemetery to see the excellent visitors center. Don't be afraid to take charge of your tour if you have other specific interests (some guides can get lost in battle minutiae that you don't have time for). Many tours prefer to pick up in or near Bayeux, and a few levy a small surcharge for a Caen pickup. While some companies discourage children, others embrace them.

Scheduled Tours

The following guides accept individual sign-ups for their scheduled departures.

D-Day Historian Tours are run by Paul Woodadge, a passionate historian and teacher who takes your learning seriously. He offers regularly scheduled tours in his minivan several days a week

(€85/day) and also gives private tours. His "Band of Brothers Tour" is excellent (tel. 02 31 22 28 82, www.ddayhistorian.com, paul@ddayhistorian.com).

Paul de Winter is clean-cut, serious about teaching, has a PhD in military history, and has written a book titled *Defeating Hitler*. History buffs will be happy, but so will others as Paul's delightful wife and driver, Fiona, helps balance the conversation (€70/half-day, €95/day, 6-person maximum, private tours available, www.dewintertours.com, info@dewintertours.com).

Normandy Sightseeing Tours delivers a French perspective through the voices of its small fleet of licensed guides. They take individual sign-ups and private groups (€45-morning tour, €60-afternoon tour, €90-all-day tour), and will pick you up anywhere you like (for a price). Because there are many guides, the quality of their teaching is less consistent—guides David, Olivier, and Karinne get the best reviews but only do private tours (tel. 02 31 51 70 52, www.normandy-sightseeing-tours.com, frederic-guerin@wanadoo.fr).

Vanessa Letourneur and her colleague **Sabrina** are capable, likable French natives who can guide anywhere in Normandy. Vanessa, who worked at the Caen Memorial Museum for years, offers half-day tours from Bayeux or Caen for €60/person (mobile 06 98 95 89 45, www.normandypanorama.com).

The **Caen Memorial Museum** runs a busy program of half-day tours covering the American and Canadian sectors in combination with a visit to the museum. This option works well for those who have limited time. The museum has many guides (some good, some mediocre) and is more likely to have availability when others don't.

Private Tours

The following guides offer tours only for private parties.

Dale Booth is a fine historian and a riveting storyteller. He leads tours for up to eight people to the American, Canadian, and British sectors using your vehicle or his (tel. 02 33 71 53 76, www.dboothnormandytours.com, dboothholidays@sfr.fr).

D-Day Battle Tours are run by WWII enthusiast Ellwood von Seibold. He drives a WWII Dodge Command Car, lives in a home where an American paratrooper landed in the garden, and owns a café in Ste-Mère Eglise (C-47 Café) that has the rudder of a WWII-era C-47 transport plane as its centerpiece. He lives this stuff and can

explain the events as if you were there (tel. 02 33 94 44 13, mobile 06 32 67 49 15, www.ddaybattletours.com, ellwood@ddaybattletours.com).

Normandy Battle Tours are led by likable, easygoing Stuart Robertson, who loves teaching visitors about the landings. He also owns a bed-and-breakfast near Ste-Mère Eglise and offers combo accommodation/tour packages (tel. 02 33 41 28 34, www.normandybattletours.com, stuart@normandybattletours.com).

Michael Phillips has been guiding for 16 years and brings a gentle, personal perspective to his tours. He is easy to be with and specializes in private tours (British mobile 0780-246-8599, from France dial 00-44/780-246-8599, www.d-daytours.com, info@d-daytours.com).

Edward Robinson, Irish, informal, and chatty (a national trait?), has previously guided for the Caen Memorial Museum and knows his way around the beaches. He does a terrific tour of the Omaha Beach sector (particularly Pointe du Hoc) and fires important information at you like a machine gun. Taking up to six passengers in his minivan, he tailors each tour to his clients' needs and tries to get off the beaten track (www.battleofnormandytours.com, edrobinson@battleofnormandytours.com).

Eva Ruttger is young, smart, and energetic. She was raised in Germany and can speak to that perspective when touring the beaches. She offers full- and half-day tours in an eight-person minivan, or will join your car for less. For a multi-day tour, she can pick you up in Paris and guide in Giverny, Honfleur, or other towns on the way to the D-Day beaches (mobile 06 50 48 68 19, www.visitnormandybeaches.com, info@visitnormandybeaches.com).

Victory Tours is run by friendly Dutchman Roel (pronounced "rule"), who gives half-day, all-day, and two-day tours. His tours are informal and entertaining, but sufficiently informative for most (departs from Bayeux only, tel. 02 31 51 98 14, www.victorytours.com, victorytours@orange.fr).

Lucie Hoffmann, hip, relaxed, and French, has been guiding for 10 years throughout Normandy. Having worked for four years at the Caen Memorial Museum, she knows her WWII history. She also loves guiding kids (mobile 06 03 09 10 21, luciehoffmann@msn.com).

Mathias Leclere brings a thoughtful, French perspective to his tour. Born four miles from Juno Beach to a family with three centuries of roots in Normandy, he is part of its soil. Mathias is a self-taught historian who leads half- and full-day tours in his minivan (www.ddayguidedtours.com).

Countdown to D-Day

1939   On September 1, Adolf Hitler invades the Free City of Danzig (today's Gdańsk, Poland), sparking World War II.

1940   Germany's "Blitzkrieg" ("lightning war") quickly overwhelms France, Nazis goose-step down the Avenue des Champs-Elysées, and the country is divided into Occupied France (the north) and Vichy France (the south, ruled by right-wing French). Just like that, nearly the entire Continent is fascist.

1941   The Allies (Britain, the Soviet Union, and others) peck away at the fringes of "fortress Europe." The Soviets repel Hitler's invasion at Moscow, while the Brits (with American aid) battle German U-boats for control of the seas. On December 7, Japan bombs the US naval base at Pearl Harbor, Hawaii. The US enters the war against Japan and its ally, Germany.

1942   Three crucial battles—at Stalingrad, El-Alamein, and Guadalcanal—weaken the German forces and their ally Japan. The victorious tank battle at El-Alamein in the deserts of North Africa soon gives the Allies a jumping-off point (Tunis) for the first assault on the Continent.

1943   More than 150,000 Americans and Brits, under the command of George Patton and Bernard "Monty" Montgomery, land in Sicily and begin working their way north through Italy. Meanwhile, Germany has to fend off tenacious Soviets on their eastern front.

1944   On June 6, 1944, the Allies launch "Operation Overlord," better known as D-Day. The Allies amass three million soldiers and six million tons of *matériel* in England in preparation for the biggest fleet-led invasion in history—across the English Channel to France, then eastward toward Berlin. The Germans, hunkered down

Helpful Hints

Normandy Pass: If you plan to visit several D-Day sites, you can save a few euros by buying the Normandy Pass (€1 added to the full-price admission at your first site). You'll save €1 at most subsequent sites, but the Caen Memorial Museum is not included. The pass is valid for one month and is transferrable to anyone.

Good Map: The free and well-done *Exploration and Emotion: The Historical Area of the Battle of Normandy* booklet gives succinct reviews of 29 D-Day museums and sites with curin northern France, know an invasion is imminent, but the Allies keep the details top secret. On the night of June 5, 150,000 soldiers board ships and planes, not knowing where they are headed until they're under way. Each one carries a note from General Dwight D. Eisenhower: "The tide has turned. The free men of the world are marching together to victory."

At 6:30 on June 6, 1944, Americans spill out of troop transports into the cold waters off a beach in Normandy, code-named Omaha. The weather is bad, seas are rough, and the prep bombing has failed. The soldiers, many seeing their first action, are dazed, confused, and weighed down by heavy packs. Nazi machine guns pin them against the sea. Slowly, they crawl up the beach on their stomachs. More than a thousand die. They hold on until the next wave of transports arrives.

Americans also see action at Utah Beach, while the British and Canadian troops storm Sword, Juno, and Gold. All day long, Allied confusion does battle with German indecision—the Nazis never really counterattack, thinking D-Day is just a ruse, not the main invasion. By day's end, the Allies take several beaches along the Normandy coast and begin building artificial harbors, providing a tiny port-of-entry for the reconquest of Europe. The stage is set for a quick and easy end to the war. Right.

1945 Having liberated Paris (August 26, 1944), the Allies' march on Berlin from the west bogs down, hit by poor supply lines, bad weather, and the surprising German counterpunch at the Battle of the Bulge. Finally, in the spring, the Americans and Brits cross the Rhine, Soviet soldiers close in on Berlin, Hitler shoots himself, and—after nearly six long years of war—Europe is free.

rent opening times. It also mentions driving itineraries that are linked to roadside signposts, helping you understand the significance of the area you are passing through. The map is available at TIs, but you usually need to ask for it (or you can download it yourself from www.normandiememoire.com).

Food Strategies: The D-Day landing sites are rural, and you won't find a restaurant or grocery on every corner. This is the time to pack that perfect French picnic. Especially if you are traveling with kids, load up on snacks and beverages before heading out. Otherwise, consider timing your lunch to coincide with your visit to Omaha Beach, where you'll find recommended restaurants nearby.

Arromanches

This small town was ground zero for the D-Day invasion. Almost overnight, it sprouted the immense harbor, Port Winston, which gave the Allies a foothold in Normandy, allowing them to begin their victorious push to Berlin and end World War II. The postwar period brought a long decline. Only recently has the population of tiny Arromanches finally returned to its June 5, 1944, numbers. Here you'll find a good museum, an evocative beach and bluff, and a touristy-but-fun little town that offers a pleasant cocktail of war memories, cotton candy, and beachfront trinket shops. Arromanches makes a great base for sightseeing (I've listed accommodations under "Sleeping in Arromanches," later). Sit on the seawall after dark and listen to the waves lick the sand while you contemplate the events that took place here 70 years ago.

Orientation to Arromanches

Tourist Information

The TI has the *Exploration and Emotion* booklet, bus schedules, a photo booklet of area hotels, and a list of *chambres d'hôtes* (daily June-Aug 9:30-19:00, Sept-May 9:30-12:30 & 14:00-16:30, opposite the recommended Hôtel d'Arromanches at 2 Avenue Maréchal Joffre, tel. 02 31 22 36 45, www.ot-arromanches.fr).

Arrival in Arromanches

The main parking lot by the museum costs €1 per hour. For free parking and less traffic, look for the lot between the small grocery store and Ideale Hôtel Mountbatten as you enter Arromanches.

Helpful Hints

ATM: Across the street from the museum parking lot, you'll find an ATM run by the French postal system.

Groceries: A little **supermarket** is a few blocks above the beach, across from the Ideale Hôtel Mountbatten.

Taxi: To get an Arromanches-based **taxi,** call mobile 06 66 62 00 99.

D-Day Sites in Arromanches

In this section, I've linked Arromanches' D-Day sites with some self-guided commentary.

▲▲▲Port Winston Artificial Harbor

Start on the cliffs above the town, overlooking the site of the impressive WWII harbor.

NORMANDY

Getting There: Drive two minutes toward Courseulles-sur-Mer and pay €3 to park, or park in Arromanches and walk up. Non-drivers can hike 10 minutes uphill from Arromanches, or take the free white train from the museum to the top of the bluff (runs daily June-Sept, Sat-Sun only Oct-May).

❍ **Self-Guided Tour:** This commentary will lead you around the site.

• *Find the concrete viewpoint overlooking the town and the beaches and prepare for your briefing. Beyond Arromanches to the left is the American sector, with Omaha Beach and then Utah Beach (notice the sheer cliffs); below and to the right lie the British and Canadian sectors (more level terrain).*

Now get this: Along the beaches below, the Allies arrived in the largest amphibious attack ever, launching the liberation of Western Europe. On D-Day +1—June 7, 1944—17 old ships sailed 90 miles across the English Channel under their own steam to Arromanches. Their crews sank them so that each bow faced the next ship's stern, forming a sea barrier. Then 500 tugboats towed 115 football-field-size cement blocks (called "Mulberries") across the channel. These were also sunk, creating a four-mile-long breakwater 1.5 miles offshore. Finally, engineers set up seven floating steel "pierheads" with extendable legs; they then linked these to shore with four mile-long floating roads made of concrete pontoons. Soldiers placed anti-aircraft guns on the Mulberries and pontoons, protecting a port the size of Dover, England. Within just six days of operation, 54,000 vehicles, 326,000 troops, and 110,000 tons of goods had crossed the English Channel. An Allied toehold in Normandy was secure. Eleven months later, Hitler was dead and the war was over.

The **Arromanches 360° Theater** behind you shows a moving film, *Normandy's 100 Days*, encompassing D-Day and the ferocious battle to liberate Normandy. It flashes back and forth from quiet farmlands and beaches to the summer of 1944. It's a noisy montage of videos on a 360° screen—stand as near to the center as you can (€4.90, daily mid-Feb-Dec 10:00-18:00, until 18:30 June-Aug; closed Jan-mid-Feb, 2 shows/hour at :10 and :40 past the hour, 20 minutes, tel. 02 31 06 06 45, www.arromanches360.com).

• *Head down to the town's main parking lot and find the round bulkhead on the seawall, near the D-Day Landing Museum entry. Stand facing the sea.*

The world's first prefab harbor was created out there by the British. Since it was Churchill's brainchild, it was named Port Winston. Designed to be a temporary harbor (it was used for six months), it was supposed to wash out to sea over time—which is exactly what happened with its twin harbor at Omaha Beach (that one lasted only 12 days, thanks to a terrible storm). If the tide is out, you'll see several rusted floats mired on the sand close in—these supported the pontoon roads. If you stare hard enough at the concrete blocks in the sea to the right, you'll see that one still has what's left of an anti-aircraft gun on it. On the hill beyond the museum, you'll spot a Sherman tank, one of 50,000 deployed during the landings. Behind the museum (not viewable from here) you'll find a section of a pontoon road, an anti-aircraft gun, and a Higgins boat, which was used to ferry 36 soldiers at a time from naval ships to the beaches. If you can, walk down to the beach and wander among the concrete and rusted litter of the battle—and be thankful that all you hear are birds and surf.

▲D-Day Landing Museum (Musée du Débarquement)

The D-Day Landing Museum, facing the harbor, makes a worth-while 45-minute visit and is the only way to get a full appreciation of how the artificial harbor was built. While gazing through windows at the site of this amazing endeavor, you can study helpful models, videos, and photographs illustrating the construction and use of the prefabricated harbor. Those blimp-like objects tethered to the port prevented German planes from getting too close (though the German air force had been made largely irrelevant by this time). Ponder the remarkable undertaking that resulted in this harbor being built in just 12 days, while battles raged. One video (8 minutes, ground floor) recalls D-Day; the other (15 minutes, upstairs) features the construction of the temporary port—ask for times when it is shown in English.

Cost and Hours: €7.50, daily May-Aug 9:00-19:00, Sept 9:00-18:00, Oct-Dec and Feb-April 10:00-12:30 & 13:30-17:00, closed Jan, pick up English flier at door, tel. 02 31 22 34 31, www.arromanches-museum.com.

Sleeping in Arromanches

Arromanches, with its pinwheels and seagulls, has a salty beach-town ambience that makes it a good overnight stop. Park in the town's main lot at the museum (€1/hour, free 19:00-9:00). For evening fun, do what most do and head for the small bar at **Restaurant "Le Pappagall"** (see "Eating in Arromanches"), or, for more of a nightclub scene, have a drink at **Pub Marie Celeste,** around the corner on Rue de la Poste. Drivers should also consider my sleeping recommendations near Omaha Beach.

$$$ Hôtel de la Marine* has one of the best locations for D-Day enthusiasts, with point-blank views to the artificial harbor site from most of its 28 comfortable and non-smoking rooms (Db-€116, Tb-€150, Qb-€175, bigger family rooms, includes breakfast, elevator, Wi-Fi, view restaurant, half-board strongly encouraged—

figure €85/person, Quai du Canada, tel. 02 31 22 34 19, www.
hotel-de-la-marine.fr, hotel.de.la.marine@wanadoo.fr).

$$ Hôtel d'Arromanches**, which sits on the main pedestrian
drag near the TI, is a fine value, with nine mostly small but smartly
appointed rooms (some with water views), all up a tight stairway.
Here you'll find the cheery, recommended Restaurant "Le Pappa-
gall" and English-speaking Louis at the helm (Db-€67, Tb-€76,
breakfast-€10, Wi-Fi, 2 Rue Colonel René Michel, tel. 02 31 22 36
26, www.hoteldarromanches.fr, reservation@hoteldarromanches.fr).

$$ Le Mulberry** is an intimate place with nine handsome
rooms and a small restaurant, just a five-minute walk up from the
touristy beach. Since it's near the town's church, expect bells to
mark the hour until 22:00 (Db-€83-105, Tb-€105-150, includes
breakfast, reception closed 13:00-17:00 and after 19:00, a block
below the church at 6 Rue Maurice Lihare, tel. 02 31 22 36 05,
www.lemulberry.fr, mail@lemulberry.fr).

$$ Ideale Mountbatten Hôtel**, located a long block up from
the water, is an eight-room, two-story, motel-esque place with gen-
erously sized, clean, and good-value lodgings. Upstairs rooms have
a little view over the sea (Db-€82, Tb-€101, includes breakfast,
Wi-Fi, easy and free parking, short block below the main post of-
fice—PTT—at 20 Boulevard Gilbert Longuet, tel. 02 31 22 59 70,
www.hotelmountbatten.com, mountbattenhotel@wanadoo.fr).

In the Countryside near Arromanches

$$ Le Mas Normand, 10 minutes east of Arromanches in Ver-
sur-Mer, is the child of *Provençale* Mylène and *Normand* Christian.
Here you get a warm welcome and the best of both worlds: four
lovingly decorated, Provence-style rooms wrapped in 18th-century
Norman stone. There's a lovely yard with ample grass, a dog, some
geese, and no smoking (Db-€75-95, Tb-€120, Qb-€140, includes
breakfast, Wi-Fi; drive to the east end of little Ver-sur-Mer, turn
right at Hôtel P'tit Bouchon, take another right where the road
makes a "T," and find the sign at 8 Impasse de la Rivière; tel. 02
31 21 97 75, www.lemasnormand.com, lemasnormand@wanadoo.
fr). Book ahead for Christian's home-cooked gourmet dinner, including wine, cider, and coffee (€35/person, requires 4 people, kids'
menus available).

$ At André and Madeleine Sebire's B&B, you'll experience
a real Norman farm. The hardworking owners offer four modest,
homey, and dirt-cheap rooms in the middle of nowhere (Sb-€35,
Db-€40, Tb-€45, includes breakfast, 2 miles from Arromanches in
the tiny village of Ryes at Ferme du Clos Neuf, tel. 02 31 22 32 34,
emmanuelle.sebire@wanadoo.fr, little English spoken). Try these
directions: Follow signs into Ryes, then locate the faded green

Chambres d'Hôte sign opposite the village's lone restaurant. Follow that sign onto Rue de la Forge, cross a tiny bridge, turn right onto Rue de la Tringale, and follow it for a half-mile until you see a small sign on the right to *Le Clos Neuf.* Park near the tractors.

Eating in Arromanches

You'll find cafés, *crêperies,* and shops selling sandwiches to go (ideal for beachfront picnics). The following restaurants offer reliable dining.

The lively **Le Bistro d'Arromanches,** on a short traffic-free street, has good prices and reliable, basic bistro fare (€8-12 pizza and pasta, €7-13 salads, daily, 19 Rue du Maréchal Joffre, tel. 02 31 22 31 32).

Restaurant "Le Pappagall" (French slang for "parakeet") has tasty mussels, filling fish *choucroute,* "*les* feesh and cheeps," salads, and a full offering with fair prices (€22-35 *menus,* see Hôtel d'Arromanches listing, earlier).

Lose the crowds at *crêperie* **La Ripaille,** a short block inland from the busy main drag. Sweet Sylvie will serve you a filling deep-dish crêpe with a green salad for €10 (closed Sun, 14 Rue du Colonel René Michel, tel. 02 31 51 02 31).

Hôtel de la Marine allows you to dine or drink in style on the water. The cuisine gets mixed reviews, but the view doesn't (*menus* from €19, cool bar with same views, daily, see hotel listing earlier).

Arromanches Connections

From Arromanches by Bus to: Bayeux (bus #74/#75, 3-5/day, none on Sun Sept-June, 30 minutes); **Juno Beach** (bus #74/#75, 20 minutes). The bus stop is near the main post office, four long blocks above the sea (the stop for Bayeux is on the sea side of the street; the stop for Juno Beach is on the post office side).

American D-Day Sites West of Arromanches

The American sector is divided between Omaha and Utah beaches. Omaha Beach starts a few miles west of Arromanches and has the most important sites for visitors, including the American Cemetery and Pointe du Hoc (four miles west of Omaha). Utah Beach sites are farther away (on the road to Cherbourg), and were also critical to the ultimate success of the Normandy invasion. The American Airborne sector covers a broad area behind Utah Beach and centers on Ste-Mère Eglise. You'll see memorials sprouting up all around the countryside.

Omaha Beach D-Day Sites

▲Longues-sur-Mer Gun Battery

Four German casemates (three with guns intact)—built to guard against seaborne attacks—hunker down at the end of a country road. The guns, 300 yards inland, were arranged in a semicircle to maximize the firing range east and west, and are the only original coastal artillery guns remaining in place in the D-Day region. (Much was scrapped after the war, long before people thought of tourism.) This battery was a critical link in Hitler's Atlantic Wall defense, which consisted of more than 15,000 structures stretching from Norway to the Pyrenees. The guns could hit targets up to 12 miles away with relatively fine accuracy if linked to good target information. The Allies had to take them out.

Enter the third bunker you pass. It took seven soldiers to manage each gun, which could be loaded and fired six times per minute (the shells weighed 40 pounds). Judging from the echoes you hear inside the bunker, I can only imagine the excruciating noise that was made each time the gun fired. Outside, climb above the bunker and find the hooks that were used to secure camouflage netting, making it nigh-impossible for bombers to locate them.

A lone observation bunker (look for the low-lying concrete bunker roof on the cliffs) was designed to direct the firing; field telephones connected the bunker to the gun batteries by underground wires. Walk to the observation bunker to appreciate the strategic view over the channel. From here you can walk along the glorious *Sentier du Littoral* (coastal path) above the cliffs and see Arromanches in the distance. Or enjoy beachy views by driving five minutes down to the water (continue on the small road past the parking lot).

Cost and Hours: Free and always open. The €5 booklet is helpful, but skip the €4 tour.

Getting There: You'll find the guns 10 minutes west of Arromanches on D-514. Follow *Port en Bessin* signs; once in Longues-sur-Mer, follow *Batterie* signs; turn right at the town's only traffic light.

▲▲▲WWII Normandy American Cemetery and Memorial

"Soldiers' graves are the greatest preachers of peace."
—Albert Schweitzer

Crowning a bluff just above Omaha Beach and the eye of the D-Day storm, 9,387 brilliant white-marble crosses and Stars of David glow in memory of Americans who gave their lives to free Europe on the beaches below. You'll want to spend at least 1.5 hours at this stirring site.

Cost and Hours: Free, daily mid-April–mid-Sept 9:00-18:00, mid-Sept–mid-April 9:00-17:00, tel. 02 31 51 62 00, www.abmc.gov. Park carefully, as break-ins have been a problem. You'll find good WCs and water fountains at the parking lot. Guided tours are offered a few times a day in high season—call ahead for times.

Getting There: The cemetery is just east of St-Laurent-sur-Mer and northwest of Bayeux in Colleville-sur-Mer. From route D-514, directional signs will point the way.

◐ Self-Guided Tour: Your visit begins at the impressive **visitors center.** Pass security, pick up the handout, sign the register, and allow time to appreciate the superb displays. On the arrival floor, computer terminals provide access to a database containing the story of each US serviceman who died in Normandy.

Descend one level, where you'll learn about the invasion preparations and the immense logistical challenges they presented. The heart of the center tells the stories of the individuals who gave their lives to liberate people they could not know, and shows the few possessions they died with. This adds a personal touch to the D-Day landings and prepares visitors for the fields of white crosses and Stars of David outside. The pressure on these men to succeed in this battle is palpable. There are a manageable number of display cases, a few moving videos (including an interview with Dwight Eisenhower), and a must-see 16-minute film (cushy theater chairs, on the half-hour, you can enter late).

A lineup of informational plaques provides a worthwhile and succinct overview of key events from September 1939 to June 5, 1944. Starting with June 6, 1944, the plaques present the progress of the landings in three-hour increments. Amazingly, Omaha Beach was secured within six hours of the landings.

A path from the visitors center leads to a bluff overlooking the piece of Normandy **beach** called "that embattled shore—portal of freedom." It's quiet and peaceful today, but the horrific carnage of June 6, 1944, is hard to forget. An orientation table looks over the sea. Nearby, steps climb down to the beautiful beach below. A walk on the beach is a powerful experience and a must if you are sans both car and tour. Visitors with cars can drive to the beach at Vierville-sur-Mer (see next listing).

In the **cemetery,** you'll find a striking memorial with a soaring statue representing the spirit of American youth. Around the statue, giant reliefs of the Battle of Normandy and the Battle of Europe are etched on the walls. Behind is the semicircular Garden of the Missing, with the names of 1,557 soldiers who were never found. A small metal knob next to the name indicates one whose body was eventually found—there aren't many.

Finally, wander through the peaceful and poignant sea of headstones. Notice the names, home states, and dates of death (but no birth dates) inscribed on each. Dog-tag numbers are etched into the lower backs of the crosses. During the campaign, the dead were buried in temporary cemeteries throughout various parts of Normandy. After the war, the families of the soldiers could decide whether their loved ones should remain with their comrades or be brought home (61 percent opted for repatriation).

A disproportionate number of officers are buried here, including General Theodore Roosevelt, Jr., who joined the invasion despite having a weak heart—he died from a heart attack one month after D-Day (you can find Ted's and his brother Quentin's graves along the sea, about 150 yards down, in the second grouping of graves just after the row 27 marker—look for the gold lettering). Families knew that these officers would want to be buried alongside the men with whom they fought. Also buried here are two of the Niland brothers, now famous from *Saving Private Ryan* (in the middle of the cemetery, just before the circular chapel, turn right just after the letter "F").

France has given the US permanent free use of this 172-acre

site. It is immaculately maintained by the American Battle Monuments Commission.

▲Vierville-sur-Mer and Omaha Beach

This essential detour for drivers allows direct access onto Omaha Beach. From the American Cemetery, drive west along D-514 into St-Laurent, then take a one-way loop drive along the beach, following *Vierville par la Côte* signs on D-517. As you drop down toward the beach, WWII junkies should stop at the **Omaha Beach Museum** (Musée Memorial d'Omaha Beach) parking lot. Outside the museum, you'll see a rusted metal object with several legs, called a "Czech hedgehog"—thousands of these were placed on the beaches by the Germans to foil the Allies' advance. Find the American 155 mm gun nearby, and keep this image in mind for your stop at Pointe du Hoc (this artillery piece is similar in size to the German guns that were targeted by US Army Rangers at that site). The Sherman tank is one of very few remaining along the D-Day beaches. The museum itself is skippable (€6, daily mid-May-mid-Sept 9:30-19:00, shorter hours off-season, closed mid-Nov-mid-Feb, tel. 02 31 21 97 44, www.musee-memorial-omaha.com, good 20-minute film).

A right turn along the water leads to **Le Ruquet** (where the road ends), a good place to appreciate the challenges that American soldiers faced on D-Day. The small German bunker and embedded gun protected this point, which offered the easiest access inland from Omaha Beach. It was here that the Americans would establish their first road inland.

Find your way out to the beach and stroll to the right, below the American Cemetery, to better understand the assignment that American forces were handed on June 6: You're wasted from a lack of sleep and nervous anticipation. Now you get seasick too, as you're about to land in a small, flat-bottomed boat, cheek-to-jowl with 35 other soldiers. Your water-soaked pack feels like a boulder, and your gun feels heavier. The boat's front ramp drops open, and you run for your life for 500 yards through water and sand onto this open beach, dodging bullets from above (the landings had to occur at low tide so that mines would be visible).

Omaha Beach witnessed by far the most intense battles of any along the D-Day beaches—although the war planners thought Utah Beach would be more deadly. The hills above were heavily fortified (and both the aerial bombers and the naval artillery failed to put them out of commission), and a single German machine gun could fire 1,200 rounds a minute. That's right—1,200. It's amazing that anyone survived. The highest casualty rates in Normandy occurred at Omaha Beach, nicknamed "Bloody Omaha." Though there are no accurate figures for D-Day, it is estimated that on the first day of the campaign, the Allies suffered 10,500 casualties (killed, wounded, and missing)—6,000 of whom were Americans. Estimates for Omaha Beach casualties range from 2,500 to 4,800 killed and wounded on that day, many of whom drowned after being wounded. But thanks to an overwhelming effort and huge support from the US and Royal navies, 34,000 Americans would land on the beach by day's end.

If the tide's out, you'll notice some remains of rusted metal objects. Omaha Beach was littered with obstacles to disrupt the landings. Thousands of metal poles and Czech hedgehogs, miles of barbed wire, and more than four million mines were scattered along these beaches. At least 150,000 tons of metal were taken from the beaches after World War II, and they still didn't get it all. They never will.

If your stomach is grumbling, **Hôtel La Sapinière's** airy and reasonable café is a short walk away (just west of the American Cemetery).

Back in your car, retrace your route along the beach (look for worthwhile information boards along the sea) and hug the coast past the flags heading toward the Pointe de la Percée cliff, which, from here, looks very Pointe du Hoc-like (American Army Rangers mistook this cliff for Pointe du Hoc, costing them time and lives).

A local artist made that striking metal sculpture rising from the waves in honor of the liberating forces, and to symbolize the rise of freedom on the wings of hope.

Keep hugging the coastline on D-517 and pull over about 100 yards before the Hôtel Casino to find the two German bunkers just below the hotel—now transformed into a monument to US National Guard troops who landed on D-Day. Anti-tank guns housed in these bunkers were not aimed out to sea, but instead were positioned to fire directly up the beach.

Look out to the ocean. It was here that the Americans assembled their own floating bridge and artificial harbor (à la Arromanches). The harbor functioned for 12 days before being destroyed by an unusually vicious June storm (the artificial ports at Arromanches and Utah Beach were used until November of 1944). Have a seaside drink or lunch at the casino's café, and contemplate a stroll toward the jutting Pointe de la Percée.

Drive on past the Hôtel Casino on D-517. As you climb away from the beach, look to your left and try to find two small concrete window frames high in the cliff that served German machine gun nests, and notice the pontoon bridge on the right that had been

installed at this beach. After the storm, it was moved to Arromanches and used as a second off-loading ramp. It was discovered only
a few years ago...in a junkyard.

At the junction with D-514, turn right (west) toward Pointe
du Hoc. Along the way, in the hamlet of Englesqueville la Percée,
you'll see a 10th-century fortified farm on the left offering **Calvados tastings**. To try some, cross the drawbridge, ring the rope bell,
and meet charming owners Souzic and Bernard Lebrec. Start with
their cider, move on to Pommeau (a mix of apple juice and Calvados), and finish with Calvados. They also sell various other regional
products, including D-Day Honey, which is made by one of the
guides I recommend (tel. 09 60 38 60 17, mobile 06 76 37 46 41).

▲▲▲Pointe du Hoc

The intense bombing of the beaches by Allied forces is best experi-
enced here, where US Army Rangers scaled impossibly steep cliffs
to disable a German gun battery. Pointe du Hoc's bomb-cratered,
lunar-like landscape and remaining bunkers make it one of the
most evocative of the D-Day sites.

Cost and Hours: Pointe du Hoc is free and open daily April-
Sept 9:00-18:00, Oct-March 9:00-17:00, tel. 02 31 51 62 00.

Getting There: It's off route D-514, 20 minutes west of the
American Cemetery.

Visiting Pointe du Hoc: Park near the new visitors center
and stop here first for an overview of the heroic efforts to take the
Pointe. Relax in the cinema for a 20-minute film on this Mission
Impossible assault. Then follow the path toward the sea. Upon entering the site, you'll see an opening on your left that's as wide as
a manhole cover and about six feet deep. This was a machine gun
nest. Three soldiers would be holed up down there—a commander,
a gun loader, and the gunner.

Climb to the viewing platform ahead and survey the scene.
This point of land was the Germans' most heavily fortified position
along the D-Day beaches and held six anti-ship guns capable of
firing 12 miles east to west. Omaha Beach is 11 miles to the east;
Utah Beach is seven miles to the west. For the American landings
to succeed, the Allies had to run the Germans off this cliff. So they
bombed it to smithereens, dropping over 1,500 tons of bombs on
this one cliff top. That explains the craters. Heavy bombing started
in April of 1944, continued into May, and hit its peak on June 6—
making this the most intensely bombarded site of the D-Day targets. Even so, only about 5 percent of the bunkers were destroyed.
The problem? Multiple direct hits were needed to destroy bunkers
like these, which were well-camouflaged and whose thick, dense
walls were heavily reinforced.

Walk around. The battle-scarred German bunkers and the cratered landscape remain much as the Rangers left them. You can crawl in and out of the bunkers at your own risk, but picnicking is forbidden—the bunkers are considered gravesites. Notice the six large, round open sites with short rusted poles stuck in a concrete center. Each held an anti-ship gun (picture the 155 mm gun you saw by the Omaha Beach Museum). Destroying these was the Rangers' goal.

Walk to the bunker hanging over the ocean with the stone column at its top. This memorial symbolizes the Ranger "Dagger," planted firmly in the ground. Read the inscription, then walk below the sculpture to peer into the narrow slit of the bunker. Look over the cliff, and think about the 225 handpicked Rangers who attempted a castle-style assault. They landed to your right, used ladders borrowed from London fire departments to get a head start up the cliff, and fired rockets to position their grappling hooks and climbing ropes on the cliff face. Timing was critical, as they had just 30 minutes before the rising tide would overcome the men below. Only about a third of the Rangers survived the assault. After finally succeeding in their task, the Rangers found that the guns had been moved—the Germans had put telegraph poles in their place. (Commander Erwin Rommel had directed that all coastal guns not under the cover of roofs be pulled back due to air strikes.) The Rangers eventually found the guns stashed a half-mile inland and destroyed them.

Climb down into the bunker, which was the site's communication center, and find the room with the narrow opening. From here, men would direct the firing of the six anti-ship guns via telephone. Also in the bunker are rooms where soldiers ate and slept.

▲German Military Cemetery

To ponder German losses, visit this somber, thought-provoking resting place of 21,000 German soldiers. This was the original site for the American Cemetery now on Omaha Beach. And compared to the American Cemetery, which symbolizes hope and victory, this one is a clear symbol of defeat and despair. The site seems appropriately bleak, with two graves per simple marker and dark, basalt crosses in groups of five scattered about. Birth and death dates (day/month/year) on the graves make clear the tragedy of the soldiers' short lives. The circular mound in the middle covers the remains of 207 unknown soldiers and 89 others. Notice the ages of the young soldiers who gave their lives for a cause they couldn't understand. A small visitors center gives more information on this and other German war cemeteries.

Cost and Hours: Free, daily April-Oct 8:00-19:00, Nov-March until 17:30, tel. 02 31 22 70 76.

Getting There: It's on N-13 in the village of La Cambe, 15 minutes south of Pointe du Hoc and 15 minutes west of Bayeux (follow signs reading *Cimetière Militaire Allemande*).

Sleeping near Omaha Beach

With a car, you can find better deals on accommodations and wake up a stone's throw from many landing sites. Besides these recommended spots, you'll pass scads of good-value *chambres d'hôtes* as you prowl the D-Day beaches.

$$ Hôtel la Sapinière** is a find just a few steps from the beach below the American Cemetery. A grassy, beach-bungalow kind of place, it has sharp, crisp rooms, all with private patios, and a lighthearted, good-value restaurant/bar (Db-€90, loft Db-€105, Tb/Qb-€130; breakfast-€10, in Le Ruquet in St-Laurent-sur-Mer—find it a little west of the American Cemetery by taking D-517 down to the beach, turning right, and driving almost all the way to the road's end; tel. 02 31 92 71 72, www.la-sapiniere.fr, sci-thierry@wanadoo.fr).

$$ Hôtel du Casino** is a good place to experience Omaha Beach. This average-looking hotel has surprisingly comfortable rooms and sits alone, overlooking the beach in Vierville-sur-Mer, between the American Cemetery and Pointe du Hoc. The halls have pebble walls, and all rooms have views, but the best face the sea: Ask for *côté mer*. Don't expect an effusive greeting. Introverted owner Madame Clémençon will leave you alone with the sand, waves, seagulls, and your thoughts (Db-€80, view Db-€90, extra bed-€16, view restaurant with *menus* from €27, café/bar on the beach below, tel. 02 31 22 41 02, hotel-du-casino@orange.fr). Don't confuse this with the Hôtel du Casino in St-Valery en Caux.

$ At Ferme du Mouchel, animated Odile rents four colorful and good rooms with sweet gardens in a lovely farm setting (Db-€56, Tb-€64-74, Qb-€80-90, includes breakfast, a few minutes inland in the village of Formigny, well-signed from the beaches, tel. 02 31 22 53 79, mobile 06 15 37 50 20, www.ferme-du-mouchel.com, odile.lenourichel@orange.fr).

$ La Ferme du Lavoir has two good rooms at great prices (one is a huge quad) and cider/Calvados tastings (Db-€55, Tb-€70, Qb-€85, includes breakfast, about 2 miles south of American Cemetery on Route de St-Laurent-sur-Mer in Formigny, tel. 02 31 22 56 89, www.fermedulavoir.fr, contact@fermedulavoir.fr).

Utah Beach D-Day Sites

▲▲▲Utah Beach Landing Museum (Musée du Débarquement)

This is the best museum located on the D-Day beaches, and worth the 45-minute drive from Bayeux. For the Allied landings to succeed, many coordinated tasks had to be accomplished: Paratroopers had to be dropped inland, the resistance had to disable bridges and cut communications, bombers had to deliver payloads on target and on time, the infantry had to land safely on the beaches, and supplies had to follow the infantry closely. This thorough yet manageable museum pieces those many parts together in a series of fascinating exhibits and displays.

Cost and Hours: €7.50, daily June-Sept 9:30-19:00, Oct-Nov and Feb-May 10:00-18:00, closed Dec-Jan, last entry one hour before closing, tel. 02 33 71 53 35, www.utah-beach.com. Guided museum tours are sometimes offered—call ahead or ask when you arrive (tours are free, tips appropriate).

Getting There: From Bayeux, travel west toward Cherbourg on N-13 and take the Utah Beach exit (D-913, two exits after passing Carentan). Turn right at the exit to reach the museum. An American and French flag duo leads to the entry as you approach. The road leaving the museum, the Route de la Liberté, runs all the way from Utah Beach to Cherbourg, and on to Paris and Berlin, with every kilometer identified with road markers.

Visiting the Museum: Built around the remains of a concrete German bunker, the museum nestles in the sand dunes on Utah Beach, with floors above and below sea level. Enter through the glass doors and learn about the American landings on Utah Beach, the German defenses there (Rommel was displeased at what he found two weeks before the invasion), and daily life before and after the occupation. Don't miss the display of objects American soldiers brought to the French (chewing gum, Coke, Nescafé, and good cigarettes).

The highlight of the museum are the exhibits of innovative invasion equipment and videos demonstrating how it worked: the remote-controlled Goliath mine, the LVT-2 Water Buffalo and Duck amphibious vehicles, the wooden Higgins landing craft (named for the New Orleans man who invented it), and a fully restored B-26 bomber with its zebra stripes and 11 menacing machine guns—without which the landings would not have been possible (the yellow bomb icons indicate the number of missions a pilot had flown). Take time to enter the simulated briefing room and sense the pilots' nervous energy—would your plane fly *LOW* or *HIGH?* Listen to the many videos as veterans describe how they took the beach and rushed into the interior—including testimony from Richard Winters, the leader of Easy Company in Stephen Ambrose's WWII classic *Band of Brothers*.

The stunning grand finale is the large, glassed-in room overlooking the beach, with Pointe du Hoc looming to your right. From here, you'll peer over re-created German trenches and feel what it must have felt like to be behind enemy lines. Many German bunkers remain buried in the dunes.

Church at Angoville-au-Plain

At this simple Romanesque church, two American medics (Kenneth Moore and Robert Wright) treated German and American wounded while battles raged only steps away. On June 6, American paratroopers landed around Angoville-au-Plain a few miles inland of Utah Beach and met fierce resistance from German forces. The two medics set up shop in the small church, and treated American and German soldiers for 72 hours straight, saving many lives. German patrols entered the church on a few occasions. The medics insisted that the soldiers leave their guns outside or leave the church—incredibly, they did. In the ultimate coincidence, this 12th-century church is dedicated to two martyrs who were doctors as well.

An informational display outside the church recounts the events here; an English handout is available inside. Pass through the small cemetery and enter the church. Inside, several wooden pews toward the rear still have visible bloodstains. Find the new window that honors the American medics and another that honors the paratroopers.

Cost and Hours: Free, €3 requested donation for brochure, daily 9:00-18:00.

Getting There: Take the Utah Beach exit (D-913) from N-13 and turn right, then look for the turnoff to Angoville-au-Plain.

Dead Man's Corner Museum

In 1944, the Germans used this French home as a regional headquarters. Today, a tiny museum recounts the terrible battles that took place around the town of Carentan from June 6 to 11. A swampy inlet divided Omaha and Utah beaches, and it was critical for the Americans to take this land so that the armies on each beach could unite and move forward. But the Germans resisted, and a battle that was supposed to last one afternoon endured for five days and  left more than 2,000 Americans dead. American soldiers named the road below the museum "Purple Heart Lane."

The museum is ideal for enthusiasts and best for collectors of WWII paraphernalia (but overkill for the average traveler). Every display case shows incredible attention to detail. Dutch owner/collector/perfectionist Michel Detrez displays only original material. He acquired much of his collection from American veterans who wanted their "souvenirs" to be preserved for others to see. The museum doubles as a sales outlet, with a remarkable collection of D-Day items for sale—both original items and replicas.

Cost and Hours: €6, daily 9:00-18:00 except closed Sun mid-Oct-April, tel. 02 33 42 00 42, www.paratrooper-museum.org/us/DMC.html.

Getting There: It's in St-Côme du Mont, 15 minutes south of Ste-Mère Eglise; from the N-13 highway, go two exits north of Carentan and turn left.

Ste-Mère Eglise

This celebrated village lies 15 minutes north of Utah Beach and was the first village to be liberated by the Americans, due largely to its strategic location on the Cotentin Peninsula. The area around Ste-Mère Eglise was the center of action for American paratroopers, whose objective was to land behind enemy lines in support of the American landing at Utah Beach. The **TI** has loads of information, can book minivan tours to Utah Beach sights, and rents audiovisual guides with GPS, allowing you to discover the town and beaches on your own (€8, €250 deposit, July-Aug Mon-Sat 9:00-18:00, Sun 10:00-16:00, Sept-June 9:00-13:00 & 14:00-17:30, closed Sun, 6 Rue Eisenhower, tel. 02 33 21 00 33).

For *The Longest Day* movie buffs, Ste-Mère Eglise is a necessary pilgrimage. It was around this village that many paratroopers, facing terrible weather and heavy anti-aircraft fire, landed off-target—and many landed in the town. One American paratrooper dangled from the town's church steeple for two hours (a parachute has been reinstalled on the steeple where Private John Steele's became snagged—though not in the correct corner). And though many paratroopers were killed in the first hours of the invasion, the Americans eventually overcame their poor start and managed to take the town. They played a critical role in the success of the Utah Beach landings by securing roads and bridges behind enemy lines. Today, the village greets travelers with flag-draped streets and a handful of worthwhile sights.

At the center of town, the 700-year-old **medieval church** on the town square was the focus of the action during the invasion. It now holds two contemporary stained-glass windows that acknowledge the heroism of the Allies. One features St. Michael, patron saint of paratroopers.

Don't miss the **Airborne Museum** (€7, daily April-Sept 9:00-

18:45, Oct-Dec and Feb-March 10:00-17:00, closed Jan, 14 Rue Eisenhower, tel. 02 33 41 41 35, www.airborne-museum.org). Housed in two parachute-shaped structures, its collection is dedicated to the daring aerial landings that were essential to the success of D-Day. During the invasion, in the Utah Beach sector alone, 23,000 men were dropped from planes (remarkably, only 197 died), along with 1,700 vehicles and 1,800 tons of supplies. In one building, you'll see a Waco glider (104 were flown into Normandy at first light on D-Day) that was used to land supplies in fields to support the paratroopers. Each glider could be used only once. Feel the canvas fuselage and check out the bare-bones interior. The second, larger building holds a Douglas C-47 plane that dropped parachutists, along with many other supplies essential to the successful landings.

Canadian D-Day Sites East of Arromanches

The Canadians' assignment for the Normandy invasions was to work with British forces to take the city of Caen. They hoped to make quick work of Caen, then move on. That didn't happen. The Germans poured most of their reserves, including tanks, into the city and fought ferociously for two months. The Allies didn't occupy Caen until August of 1944.

Juno Beach Centre

Located on the beachfront in the Canadian sector, this facility is dedicated to teaching travelers about the vital role Canadian forces played in the invasion, and about Canada in general. (Canada declared war on Germany two years before the United States, a fact little recognized by most Americans today.) After attending the 50th anniversary of the D-Day landings, Canadian veterans were saddened by the absence of in-formation on their contribution (after the US and Britain, Canada contributed the largest number of troops—14,000), so they generated funds to build this place (plaques in front honor key donors).

Cost and Hours: €7, €11 with guided tour of Juno Beach, daily April-Sept 9:30-19:00, Oct and March 10:00-18:00, Nov-Dec and Feb 10:00-17:00, closed Jan, tel. 02 31 37 32 17, www.junobeach.org.

Tours: The Centre's 45-minute, English-language guided tours of Juno Beach are definitely worthwhile (€5.50 for tour alone,

€11 with Centre admission; April-Oct at 10:00, 12:00, and 15:00; July-Aug nearly hourly 10:00-16:00; verify times prior to your visit).

Getting There: It's in Courseulles-sur-Mer, about 15 minutes east of Arromanches off D-514.

Visiting Juno Beach: Your visit to the Centre includes a short film, then many thoughtful exhibits that bring to life Canada's unique ties with Britain, the US, and France, and explain how the war front affected the home front in Canada. The Centre also has rotating exhibits about Canada's geography, economy, and more.

To better understand the Canadians' role in the invasion, take advantage of the Centre's eager-to-help, red-shirted "exchange students" (young Canadians who work as guides at the Centre for a 4-month period). They are great resources for what to do and see in "their" area. Be sure to ask for the hand-drawn map showing sights of interest.

The best way to appreciate this sector of the D-Day beaches is to take a tour with one of the Centre's capable Canadian guides. The tour covers important aspects of the battles and touches on the changes to the sand dunes and beaches since the war.

Nearby: When leaving the Juno Beach Centre, to the left about 400 yards away you'll spot a huge stainless steel cross. This is La Croix de Tourraine, which marks the site where General de Gaulle landed on June 14, 1944. Information plaques describe this important event, which cemented de Gaulle's role as the leader of free France.

Canadian Cemetery

This small, touching cemetery hides a few miles above the Juno Beach Centre and makes a modest statement when compared with

other, more grandiose cemeteries in this area. To me, it captures the understated nature of Canadians perfectly. Surrounded by beautiful farmland, with distant views to the beaches, you'll find graves marked with the soldiers' names and maple leaves, and decorated with live flowers or

plants in their honor. From Courseulles-sur-Mer, follow signs to *Caen* on D-79. After about 2.5 miles (4 kilometers), take the Reviers turnoff at the roundabout.

Caen

Though it was mostly destroyed by WWII bombs, today's Caen (pronounced "kahn," population 115,000) is a thriving, workaday city packed with students and a few tourists. The WWII museum and the vibrant old city are the targets for travelers, though these sights come wrapped in a big city with rough edges. And though Bayeux or Arromanches—which are smaller—make the best base for most D-Day sites, train travelers with limited time might find urban Caen more practical because of its buses to Honfleur, convenient car-rental offices near the train station, and easy access to the Caen Memorial Museum.

Orientation to Caen

The looming château, built by William the Conqueror in 1060, marks the city's center. West of here, modern Rue St. Pierre is a popular shopping area and pedestrian zone. To the east, the more historic Vagueux quarter has many restaurants and cafés in half-timbered buildings. A marathon race in honor of the Normandy invasion is held every June 8 and ends at the Memorial Museum.

Tourist Information

The TI is opposite the château on Place St. Pierre, 10 long blocks from the train station (take the tram to the St. Pierre stop). Pick up a map and free visitor's guide filled with practical information (Mon-Sat 9:30-18:30, until 19:00 July-Aug, Sun 10:00-13:00 & 14:00-17:00 except closed Sun Oct-March, drivers follow *Parking Château* signs, tel. 02 31 27 14 14, www.tourisme.caen.fr).

Arrival in Caen

These directions assume you're headed for the town's main attraction, the Caen Memorial Museum.

By Car: Finding the memorial is quick and easy. It's a half-mile off the ring-road expressway (*périphérique nord,* take *sortie* #7, look for white *Le Mémorial* signs). When leaving the museum, follow *Toutes Directions* signs back to the ring road.

By Train: Caen is two hours from Paris (12/day) and 20 minutes from Bayeux (20/day). Caen's modern train station is next to the *gare routière,* where buses from Honfleur arrive. Car-rental offices for Hertz, Avis, Europcar, and Sixt are right across the street. There is no baggage storage at the station, though free baggage storage is available at the Caen Memorial Museum. The efficient tramway runs right in front of both stations, and taxis usually wait in front. For detailed instructions on getting to the Caen Memorial Museum, see "Getting There" in the next section.

By Bus: Caen is one hour from Honfleur by express bus (2-3/day), or two hours by the scenic coastal bus (4/day direct). Buses stop near the train station.

Sights in Caen

▲▲▲Caen Memorial Museum (Le Mémorial de Caen)

Caen, the modern capital of lower Normandy, has the most thorough and by far the priciest WWII museum in France. Located

at the site of an important German headquarters during World War II, its official name is The Caen-Normandy Memorial: Center for History and Peace (Le Mémorial de Caen-Normandie: Cité de l'Histoire pour la Paix). With two video presentations and numerous exhibits on the lead-up to World War II, coverage of the war in

both Europe and the Pacific, accounts of the Holocaust and Nazi-occupied France, the Cold War aftermath, and more, it effectively puts the Battle of Normandy into a broader context.

Cost and Hours: €19, free for all veterans and kids under 10 (ask about family rates). An audioguide (€4) streamlines your visit by providing helpful background for each area of the museum. Open March-Oct daily 9:00-19:00; Nov-Dec and Feb Tue-Sun 9:30-18:00, closed Mon; closed most of Jan; last entry 75 minutes before closing, tel. 02 31 06 06 44—as in June 6, 1944, www.memorial-caen.fr.

Getting There by Taxi: Cabs normally wait in front of the train station and are the easiest solution (about €15 one-way, 15 minutes), particularly if you have bags.

Getting There by Public Transit: Allow 30 minutes for the one-way trip via tram and bus. Take the tram right in front of the station; it's the first shelter after you leave the train station—do not cross the tram tracks (line A, direction: Campus 2, or line B, direction: St. Clair; buy €1.30 ticket from machine before boarding). Your ticket is good on both tram and bus for one hour; validate it on tram—white side up—and again on the bus when you transfer. Get off at the third tram stop (Bernières), then transfer to frequent bus #2. To reach the bus stop (which is signed from the tram stop), exit the tram, cross the street to the left in front of the tram, and walk 25 feet up Rue de Bernières until you see the bus shelter for #2. For transit maps, see www.twisto.fr.

Returning from the museum by bus and tram is a snap (taxi there and bus/tram back is a good compromise). Bus #2 waits across from the museum on the street's right side (the museum has the schedule). Buy your ticket from the driver and validate it. The bus whisks you to the Quatrans stop in downtown Caen (follow the stop diagram in the bus as you go), where you'll transfer to the tram right next to the bus stop—validate your ticket again when you board. Either line A or line B will take you to the station—get off at the Gare SNCF stop.

Services: The museum provides free baggage storage and free supervised babysitting for children under 10 (for whom exhibits may be too graphic). There's a large gift shop with plenty of books in English, an excellent and reasonable all-day sandwich shop/café above the entry area, and a restaurant with a garden-side terrace (lunch only, located in the Cold War wing). Picnicking in the gardens is also an option.

Minivan Tours: The museum offers good-value minivan tours covering the key sites along the D-Day beaches. Two identical half-day tours leave the museum: one at 9:00 (€64/person) and one at 13:00 or 14:00—depending on the season (€80/person); both include entry to the museum. The all-day "D-Day Tour" package (€114, includes English information book) is designed for day-trippers and includes pick-up from the Caen train station (with frequent service from Paris), a tour of the Caen Memorial Museum followed by lunch, then a five-hour tour in English of the American sector. Your day ends with a drop-off at the Caen train station in time to catch a train back to Paris or elsewhere. Canadians have a similar €114 tour option that will take them to Juno Beach. Contact the museum for details, reservations, and advance payment.

Planning Your Museum Time: Allow a minimum of 2.5 hours for your visit, including 50 minutes for the movies. You could easily spend all day here; in fact, tickets purchased after 13:00 are valid for 24 hours, so you can return the next day. The museum is divided into two major wings: the "World Before 1945" (the lead-up to World War II and the battles and related events of the war), and the "World After 1945" (Cold War, the Berlin Wall, cartoonists on world peace, and so on). Though each wing provides stellar exhibits and great learning, I'd spend most of my time on the "World Before 1945."

The museum is amazing, but it overwhelms some with its many interesting exhibits (all well-described in English). Limit your visit to the WWII sections and be sure to read the information boards that give a helpful overview of each sub-area. Then feel free to pick and choose which displays to focus on. The audioguide provides similar context to the exhibits.

My recommended plan of attack: Start your visit with the *Jour J* movie that sets the stage, then tour the WWII sections and finish with the second movie *(Espérance).*

◐ Self-Guided Tour: Begin by watching *Jour J (D-Day),* a powerful 15-minute film that shows the build-up to D-Day itself (runs every 30 minutes from 10:00 to 18:00, pick up schedule as you enter, works in any language). Although snippets come from the movie *The Longest Day* and German army training films, some footage is of actual battle.

On the opposite side of the entry hall from the theater, find *Début de la Visite* signs and begin your museum tour with a downward-spiral stroll, tracing (almost psychoanalyzing) the path Europe followed from the end of World War I to the rise of fascism to World War II.

The lower level gives a thorough look at how World War II was fought—from General Charles de Gaulle's London radio broadcasts to Hitler's early missiles to wartime fashion to the D-Day landings. Videos, maps, and countless displays relate the war's many side stories, including the Battle of Britain, the French Resistance, Vichy France, German death camps, and the Battle of Stalingrad. To be more comprehensive, the museum has added exhibits about the war in the Pacific as well. Remember to read the information panels in each section, and then be selective about how much detail you want after that. Several powerful exhibits summarize the terrible human costs of World War II (Russia alone saw 21 million of its people die during the war; the US lost 300,000).

A separate exhibit covers just D-Day and the Battle of Normandy—enter on the main level next to the movie theater. Military buffs who expect a huge wing devoted to June 6, 1944, may be disappointed, but there are plenty of other museums in Normandy to satiate their interest (such as the excellent Utah Beach Landing Museum).

After exploring the WWII sections, try to see the second movie *(Espérance—"Hope"),* a thrilling sweep through the pains and triumphs of the 20th century (hourly, 20 minutes, good in all languages, shown in the main entry hall).

The Cold War wing sets the scene for this era with audio testimonies and photos of European cities destroyed during World War II. It continues with a helpful overview of the bipolar world that followed the war, with fascinating insights into the psychological battle waged by the Soviet Union and the US for the hearts and minds of their people until the fall of communism. The wing culminates with a major display recounting the division of Berlin and its unification after the fall of the Wall.

An exhibit labeled *Taches d'Opinion* highlights the role of political cartoonists in expressing dissatisfaction with a range of government policies, from military to environmental to human rights issues.

New in 2014 is the restoration of the German General Wilhelm Richter's command bunker next to the museum. As you tour the underground passages, you'll see exhibits on the life of German soldiers stationed along the Atlantic Wall. This wing also explores the struggles of the POWs and French citizens who built the fortifications.

The finale is a walk through the US Armed Forces Memorial Garden (Vallée du Mémorial). On a visit here, I was bothered at first by the seemingly mindless laughing of lighthearted children, unable to appreciate the gravity of their surroundings. Then I read this inscription on the pavement: "From the heart of our land flows the blood of our youth, given to you in the name of freedom." And their laughter made me happy.

Mont St-Michel

For more than a thousand years, the distant silhouette of this island abbey sent pilgrims' spirits soaring. Today, it does the same for tourists. Mont St-Michel, among the top four pilgrimage sites in Christendom through the ages, floats like a mirage on the horizon. Today, several million visitors—far more tourists than pilgrims—flood the single street of the tiny island each year.

The year 2014 is a momentous one for this timeless abbey. This is the last year for the causeway that for more than 100 years has brought tourists to Mont St-Michel's front. (It's supposed to be demolished by 2015—see "The Causeway and Its Demise" sidebar.) At the same time, a restoration of the island's ramparts may block some island walkways.

Orientation to Mont St-Michel

Mont St-Michel is surrounded by a vast mudflat and connected to the mainland by a half-mile causeway. Think of the island as having three parts: the fortified abbey soaring above, the petite village

squatting in the middle, and the lower-level medieval fortifications. The village has just one main street on which you'll find all the hotels, restaurants, and trinkets. Between 11:00 and 16:00, tourists

NORMANDY

The Causeway and Its Demise

In 1878, a causeway was built that allowed Mont St-Michel's pilgrims to come and go regardless of the tide (and without hip boots). The causeway increased the flow of visitors, but stopped the flow of water around the island. The result: Much of the bay silted up, and Mont St-Michel is no longer an island.

An ambitious project is well under way to return the island to its original form (the TI located next to the parking lot does a good job of explaining the project). Workers are replacing the causeway with a super-sleek bridge (allowing water to flow underneath). The first phase, completed in 2010, saw the construction of a dam *(barrage)* on the Couesnon River, which traps water at high tide and releases it at low tide, flushing the bay and forcing sediment out to the sea (the dam also provides great views of the abbey from its sleek wood benches). In 2011, parking near the island was removed and the mainland parking lot was built. In 2012, *navettes* (shuttles) began taking visitors from the parking lot to the island.

The entire project won't be completed until 2015. As you approach the island, expect to see cranes and busy workers. For the latest, visit www.projetmontsaintmichel.fr.

trample the dreamscape (much like earnest pilgrims did 800 years ago). A ramble on the ramparts offers mudflat views and an escape from the tourist zone. Though several tacky history-in-wax museums tempt visitors, the only worthwhile sights are the abbey at the summit of the island, and views from the ramparts and quieter lanes as you descend.

Daytime Mont St-Michel is a touristy gauntlet—worth a stop, but a short one will do. Arrive late and depart early. To avoid the tacky souvenir shops and human traffic jam on the main drag, follow the detour path up or down the mount. The tourist tide recedes late each afternoon. On nights from autumn through spring, the island stands serene, its floodlit abbey towering above a sleepy village. The abbey interior should be open until 23:00 in July and August (Mon-Sat).

The "village" on the mainland side of the causeway (called La Caserne) consists of a lineup of modern hotels and a handful of shops.

Tourist Information

An excellent TI with helpful English-speaking staff is in the new wood-and-glass building near the shuttle stop. Find the slick touch-screen monitors describing the various phases of the causeway project (daily 9:00-18:00 except until 20:00 July-Aug). Free WCs and pay baggage lockers are available.

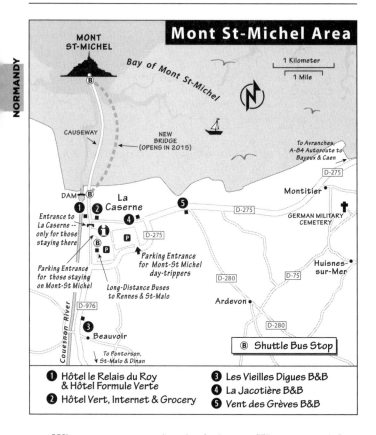

Mont St-Michel Area

1 Kilometer

1 Mile

MONT ST-MICHEL

Bay of Mont St-Michel

CAUSEWAY

NEW BRIDGE (OPENS IN 2015)

To Avranches, A-84 Autoroute to Bayeux & Caen

D-275

DAM

La Caserne

Montitier

Entrance to La Caserne -- only for those staying there

GERMAN MILITARY CEMETERY

D-275

D-275

Parking Entrance for Mont-St Michel day-trippers

Parking Entrance for those staying on Mont-St Michel

Huisnes-sur-Mer

D-280

D-75

Long-Distance Buses to Rennes & St-Malo

Ardevon

Couesnon River

D-976

Beauvoir

D-280

To Pontorson, St-Malo & Dinan

Ⓑ Shuttle Bus Stop

❶ Hôtel le Relais du Roy & Hôtel Formule Verte
❷ Hôtel Vert, Internet & Grocery
❸ Les Vieilles Digues B&B
❹ La Jacotière B&B
❺ Vent des Grèves B&B

When you arrive on the island, the tiny TI is on your left as you enter Mont St-Michel's gates. Since it's so cramped, it's smart to get your information at the TI near the parking lot. Both TIs have listings of *chambres d'hôtes* on the mainland, English tour times for the abbey, tour times for walks outside the island, bus schedules, and the tide table *(Horaires des Marées),* which is essential if you plan to explore the mudflats outside Mont St-Michel (island TI daily July-Aug 9:00-19:00, March-June and Sept-Oct 9:00-12:30 & 14:00-18:00, Nov-Feb 10:00-12:30 & 14:00-17:00; tel. 02 33 60 14 30, www.ot-montsaintmichel.com). A post office (PTT) and ATM are 50 yards beyond the TI.

Arrival in Mont St-Michel

Prepare for lots of walking, particularly if you arrive by car and are not sleeping on the island or in nearby La Caserne.

By Train: The nearest train station is in Pontorson (called Pontorson-Mont St-Michel). The few trains that stop here are met by a bus waiting to take passengers right to the gates of Mont St-

Michel (about €3, 12 buses/day July-Aug, 8/day Sept-June, fewer on Sun, 20 minutes). Taxis between Pontorson and Mont St-Michel get you to the *navette* (island shuttle) stop and cost about €20 (€30 after 19:00 and on weekends/holidays; tel. 02 33 60 33 23 or 02 33 60 82 70). If you plan to arrive on Saturday night, beware that Sunday train service from Pontorson is almost nonexistent.

By Bus: Buses from Rennes and St-Malo stop next to the *navette* stop at the parking lot (for details, see "Mont St-Michel Connections" at the end of this chapter). From Bayeux, it's faster to arrive on Hôtel Churchill's minivan shuttle.

By Car: If you're staying at a hotel on the island, follow signs for *La Caserne* and enter the gated hotel parking area—call your hotel ahead of time for the code. Those staying in La Caserne can drive right to their hotel, but you need a code number to open a gate blocking the access road (€12 access fee; get code and directions from your hotelier).

Day-trippers are directed to a sea of parking. The layout is confusing; follow the parking signs with a car icon. Take your parking ticket and pay at the machines near the TI when you leave (€12 flat fee, good for 24 hours, no re-entry privileges—if you leave and return on the same day, you'll pay another €12, machines accept cash and US credit cards, parking tel. 02 14 13 20 00).

From the remote parking lot or La Caserne village, you can either walk to the island, or take the short ride on the free shuttle (departures every few minutes). You can also ride in the horse-drawn *maringote* (double-decker wagon, €5).

Helpful Hints

Tides: The tides here rise above 50 feet—the largest and most dangerous in Europe, and second in the world after the Bay of Fundy between New Brunswick and Nova Scotia, Canada. High tides *(grandes marées)* lap against the TI door (where you'll find tide hours posted).

Internet and Groceries: The industrious **Hôtel Vert,** located in La Caserne, has a guest computer, Wi-Fi, a 24-hour grocery store, and rooms for rent (hotel described under "Sleeping in Mont St-Michel," later).

Taxi: Call 02 33 60 33 23, 02 33 60 26 89, or 06 07 96 50 36.

Guided Tours: Several top-notch guides can lead you through the abbey's complex history. The best are found in Bayeux, a good base for a day trip to Mont St-Michel. **Westcapades** provides transportation from St-Malo with minimal commentary (tel. 02 96 39 79 52, www.westcapades.com, marc@westcapades.com).

Guided Walks: The **TI** may offer guided walks of the village below the abbey (ask ahead). They also have information on inexpensive guided walks across the bay (with some English). **La Traversée Traditionelle** traces the footsteps of pilgrims, starting across the bay at Le Bec d'Andaine and walking over the mudflat to Mont St-Michel (verify that the guide speaks some English, daily April-Oct, fewer off-season, times depend on tides; €6.50, reservations recommended, 4 miles—or 1.75 hours—each way, round-trip takes 4.5 hours, including one hour on Mont St-Michel; ask at TI or call 02 33 89 80 88, www.cheminsdelabaie.com).

Crowd-Beating Tips: If you're staying overnight, arrive after 16:00 and leave by 11:00 to avoid the worst crowds. The island's main drag is wall-to-wall people from 11:00 to 16:00. Bypass this mess by following this book's suggested walking routes (under "Sights in Mont St-Michel"); the *gendarmerie* shortcut works best if you want to avoid both crowds and stairs.

Best Light: Because Mont St-Michel faces southwest, morning light from the causeway is eye-popping. Take a memorable walk before breakfast. And don't miss the illuminated island after dark (also best from the causeway).

Sights in Mont St-Michel

These sights are listed in the order by which you approach them from the mainland.

Surrounding the Island

The Bay of Mont St-Michel

The vast Bay of Mont St-Michel has long played a key role. Since the sixth century, hermit-monks in search of solitude lived here. The word "hermit" comes from an ancient Greek word meaning "desert." The next best thing to a desert in this part of Europe was the sea. Imagine the desert this bay provided as the first monk climbed the rock to get close to God. Add to that the mythic tide, which sends the surf speeding eight miles in and out with each tide cycle. Long before the causeway was built, when Mont St-Michel was an island, pilgrims would approach across the mudflat, aware that the tide swept in "at the speed of a galloping horse" (well, maybe a trotting horse—12 mph, or about 18 feet per second at top speed).

Quicksand was another peril. A short stroll onto the sticky sand helps you imagine how easy it would be to get one or both feet stuck as the tide rolled in. The greater danger for adventurers today is the thoroughly disorienting fog and the fact that the sea can encircle unwary hikers. (Bring a mobile phone.) Braving these devilish risks for centuries, pilgrims kept their eyes on the spire

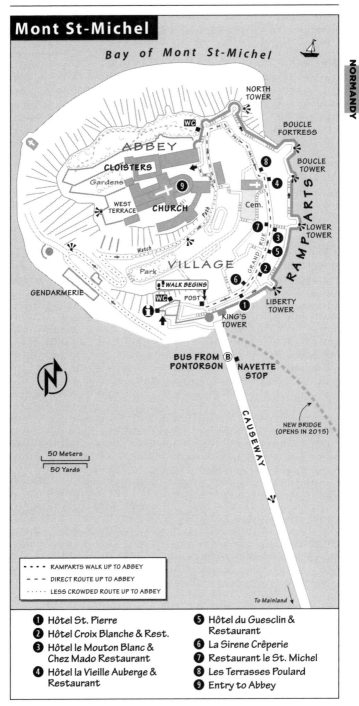

Mont St-Michel

Bay of Mont St-Michel

NORTH TOWER

BOUCLE FORTRESS

BOUCLE TOWER

WC

ABBEY

CLOISTERS

Gardens

LOWER TOWER

WEST TERRACE

CHURCH

Cem.

9

8

4

7

3

5

GRAND RUE

Path

RAMPARTS

Watch

VILLAGE

Park

2

6

WALK BEGINS

GENDARMERIE

WC POST

LIBERTY TOWER

i **1**

KING'S TOWER

BUS FROM PONTORSON **B** NAVETTE STOP

NEW BRIDGE (OPENS IN 2015)

CAUSEWAY

50 Meters

50 Yards

N

- - - - RAMPARTS WALK UP TO ABBEY
- - - DIRECT ROUTE UP TO ABBEY
· · · · · LESS CROWDED ROUTE UP TO ABBEY

To Mainland ↓

1. Hôtel St. Pierre
2. Hôtel Croix Blanche & Rest.
3. Hôtel le Mouton Blanc & Chez Mado Restaurant
4. Hôtel la Vieille Auberge & Restaurant
5. Hôtel du Guesclin & Restaurant
6. La Sirene Crêperie
7. Restaurant le St. Michel
8. Les Terrasses Poulard
9. Entry to Abbey

crowned by their protector, St. Michael, and eventually reached their spiritual goal.

▲▲Mudflat Stroll Around Mont St-Michel

To resurrect that Mont St-Michel dreamscape and evade all those tacky tourist stalls, you can walk out on the mudflats around the island (to reach the mudflats, pass through the *gendarmerie*, a former guard station, on the left side of the island as you face it). Take your shoes off and walk barefoot (handy faucets are available on your way back by the *gendarmerie*). At low tide, it's reasonably dry and a great memory-maker. But this can be hazardous, so don't go alone, don't stray far, and be sure to double-check the tides—or consider a guided walk (described under "Helpful Hints," earlier). Remember the scene from the Bayeux tapestry where Harold rescues Normans from the quicksand? It happened somewhere in this bay.

The Village Below the Abbey

Visitors usually enter the island through a stone arch at the lower left. However, during very high tides, you'll enter through the door in the central tower. The island's main street (Rue Principale, or "Grande Rue"), lined with shops and hotels leading to the abbey, is grotesquely touristy. It is some consolation to remember that, even in the Middle Ages, this was a commercial gauntlet, with stalls selling souvenir medallions, candles, and fast food. With only 30 full-time residents, the village lives solely for tourists. If crowds stick in your craw, keep left as you enter the island, passing under the stone arch of the *gendarmerie,* and follow the cobbled ramp up to the abbey. This is also the easiest route up, thanks to the long ramps, which help you avoid most stairs. (Others should follow the directions below, which still avoid most crowds.)

After visiting the TI, check the tide warnings posted on the wall and pass through the imposing doors. Before the drawbridge, on your left, peek through the door of Restaurant la Mère Poulard. The original Madame Poulard (the maid of an abbey architect who married the village baker) made quick and tasty omelets here *(omelette tradition).* These were popular for pilgrims, who, in pre-causeway days, needed to beat the tide to get out. They're still a hit with tourists—even at the rip-off price they charge today (they're much cheaper elsewhere). Pop in for a minute, just to enjoy the show as old-time-costumed cooks beat eggs.

You could continue the grueling trudge uphill to the abbey with the masses (all island hotel receptions are located on this street). But if the abbey's your goal, bypass the worst crowds and tourist kitsch by climbing the first steps on your right after the drawbridge and following the ramparts in either direction up and up to the abbey (quieter if you go right). I'd go up one way and return down the other (rampart restoration project may cause minor detours).

Public WCs are next to the island TI at the town entry, partway up the main drag, and at the abbey entrance. You can attend Mass at the tiny St. Pierre Church (times posted on the door), opposite Les Terrasses Poulard gift shop.

▲▲Abbey of Mont St-Michel

Mont St-Michel has been an important pilgrimage center since A.D. 708, when the bishop of Avranches heard the voice of Archangel Michael saying, "Build here and build high." With the foresight of a saint, Michael reassured the bishop, "If you build it... they will come." Today's abbey is built on the remains of a Romanesque church, which stands on the remains of a Carolingian church. St. Michael, whose gilded statue decorates the top of the spire, was the patron saint of many French kings, making this a favored site for French royalty through the ages. St. Michael was particularly popular in Counter-Reformation times, as the Church employed his warlike image in the fight against Protestant heresy.

This abbey has 1,200 years of history, though much of its story was lost when its archives were taken to St-Lô for safety during World War II—only to be destroyed during the D-Day fighting. As you climb the stairs, imagine the centuries of pilgrims and monks who have worn down the edges of these same stone steps. Keep to the right, as tour groups can clog the left side of the steps.

Cost and Hours: €9; May-June daily 9:00-19:00; July-Aug Mon-Sat 9:00-23:00, Sun 9:00-19:00; Sept-April daily 9:30-18:00; closed Dec 25, Jan 1, and May 1; last entry one hour before closing (www.mont-saint-michel.monuments-nationaux.fr/en). Buy your ticket to the abbey and keep climbing. Mass is held Mon-Sat at 12:00, Sun at 11:15, in the abbey church (www.abbaye-montsaint-michel.com).

Visiting the Abbey: Allow 20 minutes to hike at a steady pace from the island TI. To avoid crowds, arrive by 10:00 or after 16:00 (the place gets really busy by 11:00). In summer evenings, when the abbey is open until 23:00 and crowds are gone, visits come with music and mood lighting (€9), called *Ballades Nocturnes*. It's worth paying a second admission to see the abbey so peaceful (nighttime program starts at 19:00; daytime tickets aren't valid for re-entry, but you can visit before 19:00 and stay on).

Tours: There are no English explanations in the abbey. My self-guided tour below works for most, though the excellent audioguide gives greater detail (€4.50, €6/2 people). You can also take a 1.25-hour English-language guided tour (free but tip requested, 2-4 tours/day, first and last tours usually around 10:00 and 15:00, confirm times at TI, meet at top terrace in front of church). The guided tours, which can be good, come with big crowds. You can start a tour, then decide if it works for you—but I'd skip it, instead following my directions below.

○ Self-Guided Tour: Visit the abbey by following a one-way route. You'll climb to the ticket office, then climb some more. Stop after you pass a public WC, and look back to the church. That boxy Gothic structure across the steps is one of six cisterns that provided the abbey with water. Inside the room marked *Accueil* you'll find interesting models of the abbey through the ages.

• *Find your way to the big terrace, walk to the round lookout at the far end, and face the church.*

West Terrace: In 1776, a fire destroyed the west end of the church, leaving this grand view terrace. The original extent of the church is outlined with short walls (as well as the stonecutter numbers, generally not exposed like this—a reminder that they were paid by the piece). The buildings of Mont St-Michel are made of granite stones quarried from the Isles of Chausey (visible on a clear day, 20 miles away). Tidal power was ingeniously harnessed to load, unload, and even transport the stones, as barges hitched a ride with each incoming tide.

As you survey the Bay of Mont St-Michel, notice the polder land—farmland reclaimed by Normans in the 19th century with the help of Dutch engineers. The lines of trees mark strips of land used in the process. Today, this reclaimed land is covered by salt-loving plants and grazed by sheep whose salty meat is considered a local treat. You're standing 240 feet above sea level, at the summit of what was an island called "the big tomb." The small island just farther out is "the little tomb."

The bay stretches from Normandy (on the right as you look to the sea) to Brittany (on the left). The Couesnon River below marks the historic border between the two lands. Brittany and Normandy have long vied for Mont St-Michel. In fact, the river used to pass Mont St-Michel on the other side, making the abbey part of Brittany. Today, it's just barely—but definitively—on Norman soil. The new dam across this river (easy to see from here—it looks like a bridge when its gates are open) was built in 2010. Central to the dam is a system of locking gates that retain water upriver during high tide and release it six hours later, in effect flushing the bay and returning it to a mudflat at low tide. Walk toward the sea side of the terrace, and look down at the gardens below (where this tour will end).

• *Now enter the...*

Abbey Church: Sit on a pew near the altar, under the little statue of the Archangel Michael (with the spear to defeat dragons and evil, and the scales to evaluate your soul). Monks built the church on the tip of this rock to be as close to heaven as possible. The downside: There wasn't enough level ground to support a sizable abbey and church. The solution: Four immense crypts were built under the church to create a platform to support each of its wings. While most of the church is Romanesque (round arches, 11th century), the light-filled apse behind the altar was built later, when Gothic arches were the rage. In 1421, the crypt that supported the apse collapsed, taking that end of the church with it. Few of the original windows survive (victims of fires, storms, lightning, and the Revolution).

In the chapel to the right of the altar stands a grim-looking statue of the man with the vision to build the abbey (St. Aubert). Take a spin around the apse, and find the suspended pirate-looking ship and the glass-covered manhole (you'll see it again later from another angle).

• *After the church, enter the...*

Cloisters: A standard feature of an abbey, this was the peaceful zone that connected various rooms, where monks could meditate, read the Bible, and tend their gardens (growing food and herbs for medicine). The great view window is enjoyable today (what's the tide doing?), but it was of no use to the monks. The more secluded a monk could be, the closer he was to God. (A cloister, by definition, is an enclosed place.) Notice how the columns are staggered. This efficient design allowed the cloisters to be supported with less building material (a top priority, given the difficulty of transporting stone this high up). The carvings above the columns feature various plants and heighten the Garden-of-Eden ambience the cloister offered the monks. The statues of various saints, carved among some columns, were de-faced—literally—by French revolutionaries.

• *Continue on to the...*

Refectory: This was the dining hall where the monks consumed both food and the word of God in silence—one monk read in a monotone from the Bible during meals (pulpit on the right near the far end). The monks gathered as a family here in one undivided space under one big arch (an impressive engineering feat in its day). The abbot ate at the head table; guests sat at the table in the middle. The clever columns are thin but very deep, allowing maximum light while offering solid support. From 966 until 2001, this was a Benedictine abbey. In 2001, the last three Benedictine monks checked out, and a new order of monks from Paris took over.

• *Stairs lead down one flight to a...*

Round Stone Relief Sculpture of St. Michael: This scene depicts the legend of Mont St-Michel: The archangel Michael wanted to commemorate a hard-fought victory over the devil with the construction of a monumental abbey on a nearby island. He chose to send his message to the bishop of Avranches (St. Aubert), who saw Michael twice in his dreams. But the bishop did not trust his dreams until the third time, when Michael drove his thumb into the bishop's head, leaving a mark that he could not deny.

• *Continue down the stairs another flight to the...*

Guests' Hall: St. Benedict wrote that guests should be welcomed according to their status. That meant that when kings (or other VIPs) visited, they were wined and dined without a hint of monastic austerity. This room once exploded in color, with gold stars on a blue sky across the ceiling. (The painting of this room was said to be the model for Sainte-Chapelle in Paris.) The floor was composed of glazed red-and-green tiles. The entire space was bathed in glorious sunlight, made divine as it passed through a filter of stained glass. The big double fireplace, kept out of sight by hanging tapestries, served as a kitchen—walk under it and see the light.

• *Hike the stairs through a chapel to the...*

Hall of the Grand Pillars: Perched on a pointy rock, the huge abbey church had four sturdy crypts like this to prop it up. You're standing under the Gothic portion of the abbey church—this was the crypt that collapsed in 1421. Notice the immensity of the columns (15 feet around) in the new crypt, rebuilt with a determination not to let it fall again. Now look up at the round hole in the ceiling and recognize it as the glass manhole cover from the church altar above.

• *To see what kind of crypt collapsed, walk on to the...*

Crypt of St. Martin: This simple 11th-century Romanesque vault has minimal openings, since the walls needed to be solid and fat to support the buildings above. As you leave, notice the thickness of the walls.

• *Next, you'll find the...*

Ossuary (identifiable by its big treadwheel): The monks celebrated death as well as life. This part of the abbey housed the hospital, morgue, and ossuary. Because the abbey graveyard was small, it was routinely emptied, and the bones were stacked here.

During the Revolution, monasticism was abolished. Church property was taken by the atheistic government, and from 1793 to 1863, Mont St-Michel was used as an Alcatraz-type prison. Its first inmates were 300 priests who refused to renounce their vows. (Victor Hugo complained that using such a place as a prison was like keeping a toad in a reliquary.) The big treadwheel—the kind that did heavy lifting for big building projects throughout the Middle Ages—is from the decades when the abbey was a prison. Teams of six prisoners marched two abreast in the wheel—hamster-style—

powering two-ton loads of stone and supplies up Mont St-Michel. Spin the rollers of the sled next to the wheel.

Finish your visit by walking through the Promenade of the Monks, under more Gothic vaults, and into the vast **Scriptorium Hall** (a.k.a. Knights Hall), where monks decorated illuminated manuscripts. You'll then spiral down to the gift shop, turn right, and follow signs to the *Jardin*. The room after the shop holds temporary exhibits related to Mont St-Michel.

• *Exit the room and walk out into the rear garden. From here, look up at the miracle of medieval engineering.*

The "Merveille": This was an immense building project—a marvel back in 1220. Three levels of buildings were created: the lower floor for the lower class, the middle floor for VIPs, and the top floor for the clergy. It was a medieval skyscraper, built with the social strata in mind. The vision was even grander—the place where you're standing was to be built up in similar fashion, to support a further expansion of the church. But the money ran out, and the project was abandoned. As you leave the garden, notice the tall narrow windows of the refectory on the top floor.

• *Stairs lead from here back into the village. To avoid the crowds on your descent, turn right when you see the knee-high sign for* Musée Historique *and find your own route down or, at the same place, follow the Chemin des Ramparts to the left and hike down via the...*

Ramparts: Mont St-Michel is ringed by a fine example of 15th-century fortifications. They were built to defend against a new weapon: the cannon. They were low, rather than tall—to make a smaller target—and connected by protected passageways, which enabled soldiers to zip quickly to whichever zone was under attack. The five-sided Boucle Tower (1481) was crafted with no blind angles, so defenders could protect it and the nearby walls in all directions. And though the English conquered all of Normandy in the early 15th century, they never took this well-fortified island. Because of its stubborn success against the English in the Hundred Years' War, Mont St-Michel became a symbol of French national identity.

After dark, the island is magically floodlit. Views from the ramparts are sublime. For the best view, exit the island and walk out on the causeway a few hundred yards.

Near Mont St-Michel

German Military Cemetery (Cimetière Militaire Allemand)

Located three miles from Mont St-Michel, near tiny Huisnes-sur-Mer (well-signed east of Mont St-Michel, off D-275), this somber but thoughtfully presented cemetery-mortuary houses the remains of 12,000 German WWII soldiers brought to this location from all over France. (The stone blocks on the steps up indicate the regions in France from where they came.) A display of letters they sent home (with English translations) offers insights into the soldiers' lives. From the lookout, take in the sensational views over Mont St-Michel.

Sleeping in Mont St-Michel

Sleep on or near the island so that you can visit Mont St-Michel early and late. What matters is being here before or after the crush of tourists. Sleeping on the island—inside the walls—is a great experience for medieval romantics who don't mind the headaches associated with spending a night here, including average rooms and baggage hassles. To reach a room on the island, you'll need to carry your bags 10 minutes uphill from the *navette* (shuttle) stop. Take only what you need for one night in a smaller bag, but don't leave any luggage visible in your car.

Hotels near the island in La Caserne are a good deal cheaper and require less walking—you can park right at your hotel. All are a short walk from the free and frequent shuttle to the island, allowing easy access at any time.

On the Island

There are eight small hotels on the island, and because most visitors day-trip here, finding a room is generally no problem (but finding an elevator is). Though some pad their profits by requesting that guests buy dinner from their restaurant, *requiring* it is illegal. Higher-priced rooms generally have bay views. Several hotels are closed from November until Easter.

The following hotels are listed in order of altitude; the first hotels are lowest.

$$$ Hôtel St. Pierre*** and **Hôtel Croix Blanche*****, which share the same owners and reception desk, sit side by side (reception at St. Pierre). Each provides comfortable rooms at inflated prices, some with good views. Both have several family loft rooms (non-view Db-€170-190, view Db-€210-225, Tb or Qb-€220-280; lower rates are for Hôtel Croix Blanche, higher rates for Hôtel St. Pierre; breakfast-€15, guest computer, Wi-Fi, tel. 02 33 60 14 03, www.auberge-saint-pierre.fr, contact@auberge-saint-pierre.fr).

$$$ Hôtel le Mouton Blanc** delivers a fair midrange value, with 15 rooms split between two buildings. The main building *(bâtiment principal)* is best, with cozy rooms, wood beams, and decent bathrooms; the more modern "annex" has cramped bathrooms (Db-€145, loft Tb-€160, loft Qb-€195, tel. 02 33 60 14 08, www.lemoutonblanc.fr, contact@lemoutonblanc.fr).

$$$ Hôtel la Vieille Auberge** is a small place with sharp rooms at fair prices (Db-€120, Tb/Qb-€150-160; spring for one of the four great terrace rooms—Db-€150, Tb-€165; breakfast-€15, check in at their restaurant, but book through Hôtel St. Pierre, listed above).

$$ Hôtel du Guesclin** has the cheapest and best-value rooms I list on the island and is the only family-run hotel left there. Rooms have traditional decor and are perfectly comfortable. Check in at reception one floor up; if no one's there, try the bar on the main-street level (Db-€78-93, Tb-€93-103, breakfast-€9, Wi-Fi, tel. 02 33 60 14 10, www.hotelduguesclin.com, hotel.duguesclin@wanadoo.fr).

On the Mainland

Modern hotels gather in La Caserne on the mainland. These have soulless but cheaper rooms with easy parking and many tour groups. Remember to call at least a day ahead to get the code allowing you to skip the parking lot and drive to your hotel's front door.

$$$ Hôtel le Relais du Roy*** houses tight but well-configured and plush rooms with small balconies allowing "lean-out" views to the abbey. Most rooms are on the river side and have nice countryside views (Db-€92-105, Wi-Fi, bar, restaurant, tel. 02 33 60 14 25, www.le-relais-du-roy.com, reservation@le-relais-du-roy.com).

$$ Hôtel Vert** and **Hôtel Formule Verte**,** located across the street from each other, are run by the same company. Both provide motel-esque rooms with Wi-Fi at good rates. **Hôtel Vert** is a step up in comfort (Db-€64-82, Tb-€78-90, Qb-€95-115, tel. 02 33 60 09 33); **Hôtel Formule Verte** is modern and simple (Db-€50-66, Tb-€64-82, Qb-€80-99, tel. 02 33 60 14 13). The hotels share the same website and email address (www.le-mont-saint-michel.com, stmichel@le-mont-saint-michel.com).

Chambres d'Hôtes

Simply great values, these converted farmhouses are a few minutes' drive from the island.

$$ Les Vieilles Digues, where charming, English-speaking Danielle and Kim will pamper you, is two miles toward Pontorson on the main road (on the left if you're coming from Mont St-Michel). It has a lovely garden and seven nicely furnished and homey rooms with subtle Asian touches, all with showers (but no Mont St-Michel views). Ground-floor rooms have patios on the garden (D-€75, Db-€80, Tb-€100, includes good breakfast, easy parking—and you can walk to the free shuttle at the main parking lot, Wi-Fi, 68 Route du Mont St-Michel, tel. 02 33 58 55 30, www.bnb-normandy.com, danielle.tchen@wanadoo.fr).

$$ La Jacotière is closest to Mont St-Michel and within walking distance of the regional bus stop and the shuttle (allowing you to avoid the €12 fee to park). This place may be sold by 2014, so expect some changes to the information I've given here. There are six immaculate rooms and views of the island from the backyard (Db-€70, studio with great view from private patio-€70, extra bed-€20, includes breakfast, Wi-Fi, tel. 02 33 60 22 94, www.lajacotiere.fr, la.jacotiere@wanadoo.fr). Drivers coming from Bayeux should turn off the road just prior to the main parking lot. As the road bends to the left away from the bay, look for a regional-products store standing alone on the right. Take the small lane in front of the store signed *sauf véhicule autorisé*—La Jacotière is the next building.

$ Vent des Grèves is about a mile down D-275 from Mont St-Michel (green sign; if arriving from the north, it's just after Auberge de la Baie). Sweet Estelle (who speaks English) offers five bright, big, and modern rooms with good views of Mont St-Michel and a common deck with tables to let you soak it all in (Sb-€40, Db-€50, Tb-€60, Qb-€70, includes breakfast, Wi-Fi, tel. 02 33 48 28 89, www.ventdesgreves.com, ventdesgreves@orange.fr).

Eating in Mont St-Michel

Puffy omelets (*omelette montoise,* or *omelette tradition*) are Mont St-Michel's specialty. Also look for mussels (best with crème fraîche), seafood platters, and locally raised lamb (a saltwater-grass diet gives the meat a unique taste, but beware of impostor lamb from New Zealand—ask where your dinner was raised). Muscadet wine (dry, white, and cheap) is the local wine and goes well with most regional dishes.

The menus at most of the island's restaurants look like carbon copies of one another (with *menus* from €18 to €28, cheap crêpes, and full à la carte choices). Some places have better views or more appealing decor, and a few have outdoor seating with views along the ramparts walk—ideal when it's sunny. If it's too cool to sit outside, window-shop the places that face the bay from the ramparts walk and arrive early to land a bay-view table. Unless noted otherwise, the listed restaurants are open daily for lunch and dinner.

La Sirene Crêperie offers a good island value and a cozy interior (€9 main-course crêpes, open daily for lunch, open for dinner only in summer, enter through gift shop across from Hôtel St. Pierre, tel. 02 33 60 08 60).

Hôtel du Guesclin is the top place for a traditional meal, with white tablecloths and beautiful views of the bay from its inside-only tables (book a window table in advance; see details under "Sleeping in Mont St-Michel—On the Island," earlier).

Restaurant le St. Michel is lighthearted, reasonable, family-friendly, and run by helpful Patricia (decent omelets, mussels, salads, and pasta; open daily for lunch only, may be open for dinner in summer, test its stone toilet, across from Hôtel le Mouton Blanc, tel. 02 33 60 14 37).

Chez Mado is a stylish three-story café-*crêperie*-restaurant one door up from Hôtel le Mouton Blanc. It's worth considering for its upstairs terrace, which offers the best outside table views up to the abbey (when their umbrellas don't block it). **La Vieille Auberge** has a broad terrace with the next-best views to the abbey and, so far, no big umbrellas. **La Croix Blanche** owns a small deck with abbey views and window-front tables with bay views, and **Les Terrasses Poulard** has indoor views to the bay.

Picnics: This is the romantic's choice. The small lanes above the main street hide scenic picnic spots, such as the small park at the base of the ancient treadwheel ramp to the upper abbey. You'll catch late sun by following the ramp that leads you through the *gendarmerie* and down behind the island (on the left as you face the main entry to the island). Sandwiches, pizza by the slice, salads, and drinks are all available to go at shops along the main drag. But you'll find a better selection at the modest **supermarket** located on the mainland.

Mont St-Michel Connections

By Train, Bus, or Taxi

Bus and train service to Mont St-Michel is a challenge. Depending on where you're coming from, you may find that you're forced to arrive and depart early or late—leaving you with too much or too little time on the island.

From Mont St-Michel to Paris: There are several ways to get to Paris. Most travelers take the regional bus from Mont St-Michel to Rennes or Dol-de-Bretagne and connect directly to the TGV (4/day via Rennes, 1/day via Dol-de-Bretagne, 4 hours total via either route from Mont St-Michel to Paris' Gare Montparnasse; €12.40 for bus to Rennes, €6.40 for bus to Dol-de-Bretagne; not covered by railpass, buy ticket from driver, all explained in English at www.destination-montsaintmichel.com). You can also take the 20-minute bus ride to Pontorson (see next) and catch one of a very few trains from there (3/day, 5.5 hours, transfer in Caen, St-Malo, or Rennes).

From Mont St-Michel to Pontorson: The nearest train station to Mont St-Michel is five miles away, in Pontorson (called Pontorson/Mont St-Michel). It's connected to Mont St-Michel by a 20-minute bus ride (12/day July-Aug, 9/day Sept-June, tel. 02 14 13 20 15, www.accueilmontsaintmichel.com) or by taxi (€20, €30 at night and on weekends, tel. 02 33 60 33 23 or 02 33 60 82 70).

From Pontorson by Train to: Bayeux (2-3/day, 2 hours; also see Hôtel Churchill's shuttle van service); **Rouen** (2/day via Caen, 4 hours; 4/day via Paris, 7 hours); **Dinan** (3/day, 1.5-2.5 hours, transfer in Dol-de-Bretagne); **St-Malo** (2/day, 1-2 hours, transfer in Dol-de-Bretagne); **Amboise** (2-3/day; 5.5-7.5 hours via transfers in Caen and Tours, or via multiple transfers through Paris).

From Mont St-Michel by Bus to: St-Malo (1/day direct usually at 15:45, 1.25 hours, runs July-Aug daily, April-June and Sept-Oct Tue-Sat only, less off-season, must pay €20 round-trip fare even if only going one way, buy ticket from driver); **Rennes** (4/day direct, 1.75 hours). Keolis buses provide service to St-Malo and Rennes (tel. 02 99 19 70 70, www.keolis-emeraude.com/en).

Taxis are more expensive, but are helpful when trains and buses don't cooperate. Figure €90 from Mont St-Michel to St-Malo, and €100 to Dinan (50 percent more on Sun and at night).

By Car

From Mont St-Michel to St-Malo, Brittany: The direct (and free) freeway route takes 40 minutes. For a scenic drive into Brittany, take the following route: Head to Pontorson, follow *D-19* signs to St-Malo, then look for *St. Malo par la Côte* and join D-797, which leads along *La Route de la Baie* to D-155 and on to the oyster capital of Cancale. In Cancale, keep tracking *St. Malo par la Côte* and *Route de la Baie* signs. You'll be routed through the town's port (good lunch stop), then emerge on D-201. Take time to savor Pointe du Grouin, then continue west on D-201 as it hugs the coast to St-Malo. If continuing on to Dinan: From St-Malo, signs direct you to Rennes, then Dinan. This drive adds about 2.5 hours (with stops; takes longer on weekends and in summer) to the fastest path between Mont St-Michel

and Dinan, but is well worth it when skies are clear.

From Mont St-Michel to Bayeux: Take the free and zippy A-84 toward Caen, exit at Villers-Bocage, then follow signs to Bayeux.

PRACTICALITIES

This section covers just the basics on traveling in France (for much more information, see the latest edition of *Rick Steves' France*). You can find free advice on specific topics at www.ricksteves.com/tips.

The Language

In France, it's essential to acknowledge the person before getting down to business. Start any conversation, or enter any shop, by saying: *"Bonjour, madame (*or *monsieur)."* To ask if they speak English, say, *"Parlez-vous anglais?",* and hope they speak more English than you speak French. See "Survival Phrases" at the end of this chapter.

Money

France uses the euro currency: 1 euro (€) = about $1.30. To convert prices in euros to dollars, add about 30 percent: €20 = about $26, €50 = about $65. (Check www.oanda.com for the latest exchange rates.)

The standard way for travelers to get euros is to withdraw money from ATMs (which locals call a *distributeur*) using a debit or credit card, ideally with a Visa or MasterCard logo. Before departing, call your bank or credit-card company: Confirm that your card(s) will work overseas, ask about international transaction fees, and alert them that you'll be making withdrawals in Europe. Also ask for the PIN number for your credit card in case it'll help you use Europe's "chip-and-PIN" payment machines (see below); allow time for your bank to mail your PIN to you. To keep your valuables safe, wear a money belt.

Dealing with "Chip and PIN": Much of Europe—including France—is adopting a "chip-and-PIN" system for credit cards, and some merchants rely on it exclusively. European chip-and-

PIN cards are embedded with an electronic chip, in addition to the magnetic stripe used on our American-style cards. This means that your credit (and debit) card might not work at automated payment machines, such as those at train and subway stations, toll roads, parking garages, luggage lockers, and self-serve gas pumps. Memorizing your credit card's PIN lets you use it at some chip-and-PIN machines—just enter your PIN when prompted. If a payment machine won't take your card, look for a machine that takes cash or see if there's a cashier nearby who can process your transaction. Often the easiest solution is to pay for your purchases with cash you've withdrawn from an ATM using your debit card (Europe's ATMs still accept magnetic-stripe cards).

Phoning

Smart travelers use the telephone to reserve or reconfirm rooms, reserve restaurants, get directions, research transportation connections, confirm tour times, phone home, and lots more.

To call France from the US or Canada: Dial 011-33 and then the local number, omitting the initial zero. (The 011 is our international access code, and 33 is France's country code.)

To call France from a European country: Dial 00-33 followed by the local number, omitting the initial zero. (The 00 is Europe's international access code.)

To call within France: Just dial the local number (including the initial zero).

To call from France to another country: Dial 00 followed by the country code (for example, 1 for the US or Canada), then the area code and number. If you're calling European countries whose phone numbers begin with 0, you'll usually have to omit that 0 when you dial.

Tips on Phoning: A mobile phone—whether an American one that works in France, or a European one you buy when you arrive—is handy, but can be pricey. If traveling with a smartphone, switch off data-roaming until you have free Wi-Fi. With Wi-Fi, you can use your smartphone to make free or inexpensive domestic and international calls by taking advantage of a calling app such as Skype or FaceTime.

To make cheap international calls from any phone (even your hotel-room phone), you can buy an international phone card (*carte à code*; pronounced cart ah code). These work with a scratch-to-reveal PIN code, allow you to call home to the US for pennies a minute, and also work for domestic calls.

Another option is buying an insertable phone card (*télécarte*; tay-lay-kart). These are usable only at pay phones, are reasonable for making calls within the country, and work for international calls as well (though not as cheaply as the international phone

From:	rick@ricksteves.com
Sent:	Today
To:	info@hotelcentral.com
Subject:	Reservation request for 19-22 July

Dear Hotel Central,

I would like to reserve a room for 2 people for 3 nights, arriving 19 July and departing 22 July. If possible, I would like a quiet room with a double bed and a bathroom inside the room.

Please let me know if you have a room available and the price.

Thank you!
Rick Steves

cards). However, phone booths can be few and far between in France. Also note that insertable phone cards—and most international phone cards—work only in the country where you buy them.

Calling from your hotel-room phone is usually expensive, unless you use an international phone card. For much more on phoning, see www.ricksteves.com/phoning.

Making Hotel Reservations

To ensure the best value, I recommend reserving rooms in advance, particularly during peak season. Email the hotelier with the following key pieces of information: number and type of rooms; number of nights; date of arrival; date of departure; and any special requests. (For a sample form, see the sidebar.) Use the European style for writing dates: day/month/year. Hoteliers typically ask for your credit-card number as a deposit.

Given the economic downturn, hoteliers may be willing to make a deal—try emailing several hotels to ask for their best price. In general, hotel prices can soften if you do any of the following: offer to pay cash, stay at least three nights, or travel off-season.

The French have a simple hotel-rating system based on amenities (zero through five stars, indicated in this book by * through *****). Two-star hotels are my mainstay. Other accommodation options include bed-and-breakfasts (*chambres d'hôtes*, usually more affordable than hotels), hostels, campgrounds, or even homes (*gîtes*, rented by the week).

Eating

The cuisine is a highlight of any French adventure. It's sightseeing for your palate. For a formal meal, go to a restaurant. If you want the option of lighter fare (just soup or a sandwich), head for a café or brasserie instead.

French restaurants usually open for dinner at 19:00 and are typically most crowded around 20:30. Last seating is usually about 21:00 or 22:00 (earlier in villages). If a restaurant serves lunch, it generally goes from about 11:30 to 14:00.

In France, an entrée is the first course, and *le plat* or *le plat du jour* is the main course with vegetables. If you ask for the *menu* (muh-noo), you won't get a list of dishes; you'll get a fixed-price meal—usually your choice of three courses (soup, appetizer, or salad; main course with vegetables; and cheese course or dessert). Drinks are extra. Ask for *la carte* (lah kart) if you want to see a menu and order à la carte, like the locals do. Request the waiter's help in deciphering the French.

Cafés and brasseries provide budget-friendly meals. If you're hungry between lunch and dinner, when restaurants are closed, go to a brasserie, which generally serves throughout the day. (Some cafés do as well, but others close their kitchens from 14:00 to 18:00.) Compared to restaurants, cafés and brasseries usually have more limited and inexpensive fare, including salads, sandwiches, omelets, *plats du jour*, and more. Check the price list first, which by law must be posted prominently. There are two sets of prices: You'll pay more for the same drink if you're seated at a table *(salle)* than if you're seated or standing at the bar or counter *(comptoir)*.

A 12-15 percent service charge *(service compris)* is always included in the bill. Most French never tip, but if you feel the service was exceptional, it's kind to tip up to 5 percent extra.

Transportation

By Train: Travelers who need to cover long distances in France by train can get a good deal with a France Railpass, sold only outside Europe. Note that France is no longer offered on Eurail's Select pass. To see if a railpass could save you money, check www.ricksteves.com/rail. To research train schedules, visit Germany's excellent all-Europe website, www.bahn.com, or France's SNCF (national railroad) site, www.sncf.com.

You can buy tickets at train-station ticket windows, SNCF boutiques (small, centrally located offices of the national rail company), and travel agencies.

All **high-speed TGV trains** in France require a seat reservation—book as early as possible, as these trains fill fast, and some routes use TGV trains almost exclusively. This is especially true if you're traveling with a railpass, as TGV passholder reservations are limited, and usually sell out well before other seat reservations do.

You are required to validate (*composter*, kohm-poh-stay) all train tickets and reservations; before boarding look for a yellow machine to stamp your ticket or reservation. Strikes *(grève)* in France are common but generally last no longer than a day or two;

ask your hotelier if one is coming.

By Car: It's cheaper to arrange most car rentals from the US. For tips on your insurance options, see www.ricksteves.com/cdw, and for route planning, consult www.viamichelin.com. Bring your driver's license.

Local road etiquette is similar to that in the US. Ask your car-rental company about the rules of the road, or check the US State Department website (www.travel.state.gov, click on "International Travel," then specify your country of choice and click "Traffic Safety and Road Conditions").

France's toll road *(autoroute)* system is slick and speedy, but pricey; four hours of driving costs about €25 in tolls (pay cash, since US credit cards won't work in the machines). A car is a worthless headache in cities—park it safely (get tips from your hotel or pay to park at well-patrolled lots; look for blue *P* signs). As break-ins are common, be sure all of your valuables are out of sight and locked in the trunk, or even better, with you or in your hotel room.

PRACTICALITIES

Helpful Hints

Emergency Help: For English-speaking **police** help, dial 17. To summon an **ambulance**, call 15. To replace a passport, call the **US Consulate and Embassy** in Paris (tel. 01 43 12 22 22, 4 Avenue Gabriel, Mo: Concorde, http://france.usembassy.gov) or other **US Consulates** (Lyon: tel. 04 78 38 33 03; Marseille: tel. 04 91 54 90 84; Nice: tel. 04 93 88 89 55; Strasbourg: tel. 03 88 35 31 04; Bordeaux: tel. 05 56 48 63 85). Canadians can call the **Canadian Consulate and Embassy** in Paris (tel. 01 44 43 29 00, 35 Avenue Montaigne, Mo: Franklin D. Roosevelt, www.amb-canada.fr) or other **Canadian Consulates** (Lyon: tel. 04 72 77 64 07; Nice: tel. 04 93 92 93 22). For other concerns, get advice from your hotelier.

Theft or Loss: France has hardworking pickpockets, and they particularly target those coming in from Paris airports—wear a money belt. Assume beggars are pickpockets and any scuffle is simply a distraction by a team of thieves. If you stop for any commotion or show, put your hands in your pockets before someone else does.

To replace a passport, you'll need to go in person to an embassy or consulate (see above). Cancel and replace your credit and debit cards by calling these 24-hour US numbers collect: Visa—tel. 303/967-1096, MasterCard—tel. 636/722-7111, American Express—tel. 336/393-1111. In France, to make a collect call to the US, dial 08 00 99 00 11; press zero or stay on the line for an English-speaking operator. File a police report either on the spot or within a day or two; you'll need it to submit an insurance claim for lost or stolen railpasses or travel gear, and it can help with replacing your passport or credit and debit cards. Precautionary measures can minimize the effects of loss—back up your digital photos and other files frequently. For more information, see www.ricksteves.com/help.

Time: France uses the 24-hour clock. It's the same through 12:00 noon, then keep going: 13:00, 14:00, and so on. France, like most of continental Europe, is six/nine hours ahead of the East/West Coasts of the US.

Business Hours: Most shops are open from Monday through Saturday (generally 10:00–12:00 & 14:00–19:00) and closed on Sunday, though some grocery stores, bakeries, and street markets are open Sunday morning until noon. In smaller towns, many businesses are closed on Monday until 14:00 and sometimes all day. Touristy shops are usually open daily.

Sights: Opening and closing hours of sights can change unexpectedly; confirm the latest times with the local tourist information office or its website. Some major churches enforce a modest dress code (no bare shoulders or shorts) for everyone, even children.

Holidays and Festivals: France celebrates many holidays, which can close sights and attract crowds (book hotel rooms ahead). For information on holidays and festivals, check France's website: www.franceguide.com. For a simple list showing major—though not all—events, see www.ricksteves.com/festivals.

Numbers and Stumblers: What Americans call the second floor of a building is the first floor in Europe. Europeans write dates as day/month/year. Commas are decimal points and vice versa—a dollar and a half is 1,50, a thousand is 1.000, and there are 5.280 feet in a mile. France uses the metric system: A kilogram is 2.2 pounds; a liter is about a quart; and a kilometer is six-tenths of a mile.

Resources from Rick Steves

This Snapshot guide is excerpted from my latest edition of *Rick Steves' France,* which is one of more than 30 titles in my series of guidebooks on European travel. I also produce a public television series, *Rick Steves' Europe,* and a public radio show, *Travel with Rick Steves.* My website, www.ricksteves.com, offers free travel information, a forum for travelers' comments, guidebook updates, my travel blog, an online travel store, and information on European railpasses and our tours of Europe. If you're bringing a mobile device on your trip, you can download free information from Rick Steves Audio Europe, featuring podcasts of my radio shows, free audio tours of major sights in Europe, and travel interviews about France (via www.ricksteves.com/audioeurope, iTunes, Google Play, or the Rick Steves Audio Europe free smartphone app). You can follow me on Facebook and Twitter.

Additional Resources

Tourist Information: www.franceguide.com
Passports and Red Tape: www.travel.state.gov
Packing List: www.ricksteves.com/packlist
Travel Insurance: www.ricksteves.com/insurance
Cheap Flights: www.kayak.com
Airplane Carry-on Restrictions: www.tsa.gov/travelers
Updates for This Book: www.ricksteves.com/update

How Was Your Trip?

If you'd like to share your tips, concerns, and discoveries after using this book, please fill out the survey at www.ricksteves.com/feedback. Thanks in advance—it helps a lot.

French Survival Phrases

When using the phonetics, try to nasalize the n sound.

English	French	Pronunciation
Good day.	Bonjour.	bohn-zhoor
Mrs. / Mr.	Madame / Monsieur	mah-dahm / muhs-yur
Do you speak English?	Parlez-vous anglais?	par-lay-voo ahn-glay
Yes. / No.	Oui. / Non.	wee / nohn
I understand.	Je comprends.	zhuh kohn-prahn
I don't understand.	Je ne comprends pas.	zhuh nuh kohn-prahn pah
Please.	S'il vous plaît.	see voo play
Thank you.	Merci.	mehr-see
I'm sorry.	Désolé.	day-zoh-lay
Excuse me.	Pardon.	par-dohn
(No) problem.	(Pas de) problème.	(pah duh) proh-blehm
It's good.	C'est bon.	say bohn
Goodbye.	Au revoir.	oh vwahr
one / two	un / deux	uhn / duh
three / four	trois / quatre	twah / kah-truh
five / six	cinq / six	sank / sees
seven / eight	sept / huit	seht / weet
nine / ten	neuf / dix	nuhf / dees
How much is it?	Combien?	kohn-bee-an
Write it?	Ecrivez?	ay-kree-vay
Is it free?	C'est gratuit?	say grah-twee
Included?	Inclus?	an-klew
Where can I buy / find...?	Où puis-je acheter / trouver...?	oo pwee-zhuh ah-shuh-tay / troo-vay
I'd like / We'd like...	Je voudrais / Nous voudrions...	zhuh voo-dray / noo voo-dree-ohn
...a room.	...une chambre.	ewn shahn-bruh
...a ticket to ___.	...un billet pour ___.	uhn bee-yay poor ___
Is it possible?	C'est possible?	say poh-see-bluh
Where is...?	Où est...?	oo ay
...the train station	...la gare	lah gar
...the bus station	...la gare routière	lah gar root-yehr
...tourist information	...l'office du tourisme	loh-fees dew too-reez-muh
Where are the toilets?	Où sont les toilettes?	oo sohn lay twah-leht
men	hommes	ohm
women	dames	dahm
left / right	à gauche / à droite	ah gohsh / ah dwaht
straight	tout droit	too dwah
When does this open / close?	Ça ouvre / ferme à quelle heure?	sah oo-vruh / fehrm ah kehl ur
At what time?	À quelle heure?	ah kehl ur
Just a moment.	Un moment.	uhn moh-mahn
now / soon / later	maintenant / bientôt / plus tard	man-tuh-nahn / bee-an-toh / plew tar
today / tomorrow	aujourd'hui / demain	oh-zhoor-dwee / duh-man

PRACTICALITIES

In a French-Speaking Restaurant

English	French	Pronunciation
I'd like / We'd like...	Je voudrais / Nous voudrions...	zhuh voo-dray / noo voo-dree-oh<u>n</u>
...to reserve...	...réserver...	ray-zehr-vay
...a table for one / two.	...une table pour un / deux.	ewn tah-bluh poor uh<u>n</u> / duh
Is this seat free?	C'est libre?	say lee-bruh
The menu (in English), please.	La carte (en anglais), s'il vous plaît.	lah kart (ah<u>n</u> ah<u>n</u>-glay) see voo play
service (not) included	service (non) compris	sehr-vees (noh<u>n</u>) koh<u>n</u>-pree
to go	à emporter	ah ah<u>n</u>-por-tay
with / without	avec / sans	ah-vehk / sah<u>n</u>
and / or	et / ou	ay / oo
special of the day	plat du jour	plah dew zhoor
specialty of the house	spécialité de la maison	spay-see-ah-lee-tay duh lah may-zoh<u>n</u>
appetizers	hors d'oeuvre	or duh-vruh
first course (soup, salad)	entrée	ah<u>n</u>-tray
main course (meat, fish)	plat principal	plah pra<u>n</u>-see-pahl
bread	pain	pa<u>n</u>
cheese	fromage	froh-mahzh
sandwich	sandwich	sah<u>n</u>d-weech
soup	soupe	soop
salad	salade	sah-lahd
meat	viande	vee-ah<u>n</u>d
chicken	poulet	poo-lay
fish	poisson	pwah-soh<u>n</u>
seafood	fruits de mer	frwee duh mehr
fruit	fruit	frwee
vegetables	légumes	lay-gewm
dessert	dessert	day-sehr
mineral water	eau minérale	oh mee-nay-rahl
tap water	l'eau du robinet	loh dew roh-bee-nay
milk	lait	lay
(orange) juice	jus (d'orange)	zhew (doh-rah<u>n</u>zh)
coffee / tea	café / thé	kah-fay / tay
wine	vin	va<u>n</u>
red / white	rouge / blanc	roozh / blah<u>n</u>
glass / bottle	verre / bouteille	vehr / boo-tay
beer	bière	bee-ehr
Cheers!	Santé!	sah<u>n</u>-tay
More. / Another.	Plus. / Un autre.	plew / uh<u>n</u> oh-truh
The same.	La même chose.	lah mehm shohz
The bill, please.	L'addition, s'il vous plaît.	lah-dee-see-oh<u>n</u> see voo play
Do you accept credit cards?	Vous prenez les cartes?	voo pruh-nay lay kart
tip	pourboire	poor-bwahr
Delicious!	Délicieux!	day-lee-see-uh

For more user-friendly French phrases, check out *Rick Steves' French Phrase Book and Dictionary* or *Rick Steves' French, Italian & German Phrase Book.*

INDEX

INDEX

Rick's Free Travel App

Get your FREE **Rick Steves Audio Europe**™ app to enjoy...

- Dozens of self-guided tours of Europe's top museums, sights and historic walks

- Hundreds of tracks filled with cultural insights and sightseeing tips from Rick's radio interviews

- All organized into handy geographic playlists

- For iPhone, iPad, iPod Touch, Android

With Rick whispering in your ear, Europe gets even better.

Join a Rick Steves tour

Enjoy Europe's warmest welcome... with the flexibility and friendship of a small group getting to know Rick's favorite places and people. It all starts with our free tour catalog and DVD.

Great guides, small groups, no grumps.

See more than three dozen itineraries throughout Europe

Free information and great gear to

▶ Explore Europe

Browse thousands of articles, video clips, photos and radio interviews, plus find a wealth of money-saving tips for planning your dream trip. You'll find up-to-date information on Europe's best destinations, packing smart, getting around, finding rooms, staying healthy, avoiding scams and more.

▶ Travel News

Subscribe to our free Travel News e-newsletter, and get monthly updates from Rick on what's happening in Europe!

▶ Travel Forums

Learn, ask, share—our online community of savvy travelers is a great resource for first-time travelers to Europe, as well as seasoned pros.

Rick Steves' Europe Through the Back Door, Inc.

NOW AVAILABLE:
eBOOKS, DVD & BLU-RAY

TRAVEL CULTURE

Europe 101
European Christmas
Postcards from Europe
Travel as a Political Act

eBOOKS

*Nearly all Rick Steves guides
are available as eBooks. Check
with your favorite bookseller.*

RICK STEVES' EUROPE DVDs

11 New Shows 2013–2014
Austria & the Alps
Eastern Europe
England & Wales
European Christmas
European Travel Skills & Specials
France
Germany, BeNeLux & More
Greece, Turkey & Portugal
Iran
Ireland & Scotland
Italy's Cities
Italy's Countryside
Scandinavia
Spain
Travel Extras

BLU-RAY

Celtic Charms
Eastern Europe Favorites
European Christmas
Italy Through the Back Door
Mediterranean Mosaic
Surprising Cities of Europe

PHRASE BOOKS & DICTIONARIES

French
French, Italian & German
German
Italian
Portuguese
Spanish

JOURNALS

Rick Steves' Pocket Travel Journal
Rick Steves' Travel Journal

PLANNING MAPS

Britain, Ireland & London
Europe
France & Paris
Germany, Austria & Switzerland
Ireland
Italy
Spain & Portugal

Rick Steves®

www.ricksteves.com

EUROPE GUIDES

Best of Europe
Eastern Europe
Europe Through the Back Door
Mediterranean Cruise Ports
Northern European Cruise Ports

COUNTRY GUIDES

Croatia & Slovenia
England
France
Germany
Great Britain
Ireland
Italy
Portugal
Scandinavia
Spain
Switzerland

CITY & REGIONAL GUIDES

Amsterdam, Bruges & Brussels
Barcelona
Budapest
Florence & Tuscany
Greece: Athens & the Peloponnese
Istanbul
London
Paris
Prague & the Czech Republic
Provence & the French Riviera
Rome
Venice
Vienna, Salzburg & Tirol

SNAPSHOT GUIDES

Berlin
Bruges & Brussels
Copenhagen & the Best of
  Denmark
Dublin
Dubrovnik
Hill Towns of Central Italy
Italy's Cinque Terre
Krakow, Warsaw & Gdansk
Lisbon
Madrid & Toledo
Milan & the Italian Lakes District
Munich, Bavaria & Salzburg
Naples & the Amalfi Coast
Northern Ireland
Norway
Scotland
Sevilla, Granada & Southern Spain
Stockholm

POCKET GUIDES

Athens
Barcelona
Florence
London
Paris
Rome
Venice

Rick Steves guidebooks are published by Avalon Travel,
a member of the Perseus Books Group.

Avalon Travel
a member of the Perseus Books Group
1700 Fourth Street
Berkeley, California 94710

Portions of this book originally appeared in *Rick Steves' France 2014.*

Printed in Canada by Friesens. First printing February 2014.

ISBN 978-1-61238-687-4

For the latest on Rick's lectures, guidebooks, tours, public radio show, and public
television series, contact Europe Through the Back Door, Box 2009, Edmonds, WA
98020, 425/771-8303, fax 425/771-0833, rick@ricksteves.com, www.ricksteves.com.

Europe Through the Back Door
Managing Editor: Risa Laib
Editorial & Production Manager: Jennifer Madison Davis
Editors: Glenn Eriksen, Tom Griffin, Cameron Hewitt, Deb Jensen, Suzanne Kotz,
Cathy Lu, John Pierce, Carrie Shepherd
Editorial Assistant: Jessica Shaw
Editorial Intern: Zosha Millman
Researchers: Mary Bouron, Tom Griffin, Kristen Michel, Amy Robertson
Maps & Graphics: David C. Hoerlein, Sandra Hundacker, Lauren Mills, Mary
Rostad, Laura VanDeventer

Avalon Travel
Senior Editor and Series Manager: Madhu Prasher
Editor: Jamie Andrade
Associate Editor: Annette Kohl
Assistant Editor: Maggie Ryan
Copy Editor: Patrick Collins
Proofreader: Suzie Nasol
Indexer: Stephen Callahan
Production & Typesetting: McGuire Barber Design
Cover Design: Kimberly Glyder Design
Maps & Graphics: Kat Bennett, Mike Morgenfeld, Brice Ticen, Lohnes + Wright

Front Cover Photo: Mont St-Michel © Guillaume Dubé/ istockphoto.com
Title Page Photo: Pont du Hoc, Battlefield in WW2 during the invasion of Normandy ©
mizio1970/www.123rf.com
Page 1 Photo: Notre-Dame Cathedral in Rouen © Liudmyla Iermolenko/123rf.com
Additional Photography: Dominic Bonuccelli, Abe Bringolf, Mary Ann Cameron,
Julie Coen, Rich Earl, Barb Geisler, Cameron Hewitt, David C. Hoerlein,
Michaelanne Jerome, Lauren Mills, Paul Orcutt, Michael Potter, Carol Ries,
Steve Smith, Robyn Stencil, Rick Steves, Gretchen Strauch, Rob Unck, Laura
VanDeventer, Wikimedia Commons, Rachel Worthman, Dorian Yates.